Curriculum Visions

The River Book

SECOND EDITION

Dr Brian Knapp

White water rafting

⚠ Take care near rivers!

It is easy to visit streams and rivers to see for yourself many of the landshapes described in this book. But remember, streams and rivers can be dangerous places, so never take risks near deep water or go near a river when it is raining heavily and floods are likely.

Niagara Falls, US/Canada, is the largest waterfall in North America.

Curriculum Visions

Curriculum Visions is a registered trademark of Atlantic Europe Publishing Company Ltd.

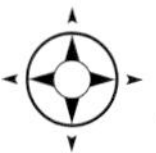

Atlantic Europe Publishing

First edition 1998.
First, second and third reprints 1998. Fourth reprint 1999. Fifth and sixth reprints 2001. Seventh and eighth reprints 2002. Ninth reprint 2003.
This second edition 2004 – includes extensive revisions.
First reprint 2005.

Author
Dr Brian Knapp, BSc, PhD

Art Director
Duncan McCrae, BSc

Senior Designer
Adele Humphries, BA, PGCE

Editors
Elizabeth Walker, BA, Mary Sanders, BA, Lisa Magloff, MA, and Gillian Gatehouse

Illustrations by
David Woodroffe

Designed and produced by
EARTHSCAPE EDITIONS

Printed in China by
WKT Company Ltd.

The River Book
– *Curriculum Visions*
A CIP record for this book is available from the British Library

Paperback ISBN 1 86214 443 5
Hardback ISBN 1 86214 445 1

Picture credits
All photographs are from the Earthscape Editions photolibrary, except the following (c=centre t=top b=bottom l=left r=right):
Prof Denys Brunsden 27tl; FEMA 35t, 35b, 38bl, 39t, 39b; Image provided by orbimage © Orbital Imaging Corporation and processing by NASA Goddard Space Flight Center 25b; NASA 23b, 25tr, 25cr, 31cr, 41t, 41br, 43br, 44tr.

This product is manufactured from sustainable managed forests. For every tree cut down at least one more is planted.

There's more on the Internet

Free information, pictures and details of our related products can be found at:

www.CurriculumVisions.com

Contents

Glossary words

There is a glossary on page 47. Glossary terms are referred to in the text by using **CAPITALS**.

Yosemite Falls, California, is the tallest waterfall in North America.

Features of rivers and valleys

These are the natural features you might expect to see in a river valley as a result of river action:

1. The **SOURCE** is the origin of a river. It may be a **SPRING** in a hillside hollow or melting snow on a mountain. The source is also known as the **HEADWATERS**. A more detailed description is on pages 8 and 9.
2. The **RIVER BASIN** (also called the drainage basin) is the whole area that is drained by a river. River basins are on page 8 and page 15.
3. Branches, or **TRIBUTARIES**, are the smaller rivers and streams that feed into the main river as shown on page 8.
4. Rivers can wear away or **ERODE** the land beneath them as shown on pages 10 and 11.
5. They can also carry material and drop, or **DEPOSIT**, it far away. Find out about this on pages 12 and 13, and also on pages 24, 25 and 31.
6. The material a river carries changes along its length. See this on pages 14 and 15.
7. A **WATERFALL** occurs where a river falls over a **CLIFF**. Find out how waterfalls work on pages 16–17.
8. A **MEANDER** is a large curve or loop in a river. Meanders are shown on pages 18 and 19.
9. Where meanders have been cut through, old channels may remain filled with water and form **OXBOW LAKES**. These are on pages 20–21.
10. In some places a **LAKE** may form where, for example, water is ponded back behind natural obstacles such as rock bars, or because land was scoured out by ancient **GLACIERS**. Find out about lakes on pages 22 and 23.
11. A **DELTA** is an area of land made by a river as it enters the sea or a lake. Deltas are shown on pages 24 and 25 together with **ESTUARIES**, which are places where a river enters the sea in a 'drowned' valley.
12. A **GORGE** or **CANYON** is a part of a **VALLEY** where the river runs between tall cliff-like sides. See this on pages 28 and 29.

⑬, ⑭ and ⑮ Rivers carve narrow valleys near their sources, but widen them out towards the sea. Find out how and why valley shapes change on pages 30–31.

16. Rivers and their valleys are home to a wide range of wildlife. Find out about river habitats on pages 32 and 33.

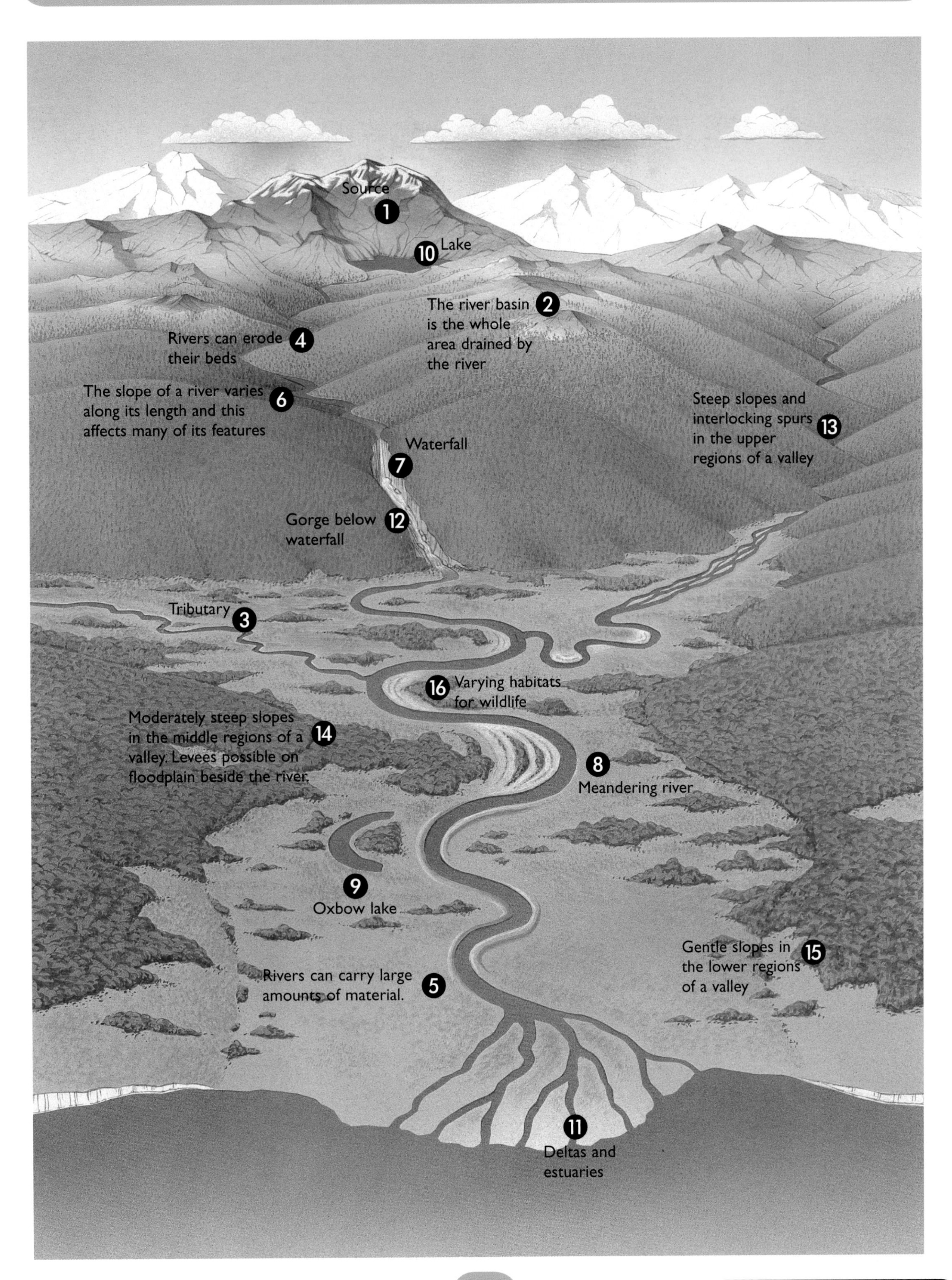

Source
1
10 Lake
The river basin is the whole area drained by the river 2
Rivers can erode their beds 4
The slope of a river varies along its length and this affects many of its features 6
Waterfall 7
Steep slopes and interlocking spurs in the upper regions of a valley 13
Gorge below waterfall 12
Tributary 3
16 Varying habitats for wildlife
Moderately steep slopes in the middle regions of a valley. Levees possible on floodplain beside the river. 14
8 Meandering river
9 Oxbow lake
Gentle slopes in the lower regions of a valley 15
Rivers can carry large amounts of material. 5
11 Deltas and estuaries

How people use rivers and valleys

These are some of the *man-made* features you might expect to see where people make use of a river and its valley.

1. Many cities were built next to rivers to carry goods or for defence. Many cities also grew up at places where the river was easy to cross, either by bridge or ferry. Unfortunately these riverside settlements are at risk from flooding. See this on page 34.

   As cities grew, so more soil was covered with houses and roads. This added to the risk of flooding. Find out why on page 36.

   Within cities, river banks are built up. This makes the river narrower and increases the chances of floods, as you will see on page 37.
2. Valley-side settlements were built to keep away from the **FLOODPLAIN**. But valley-side slopes are difficult to build on, so few of these places have grown into cities.
3. The floodplain is used for farmland because of its fertility. However, the crops may be destroyed when the land floods. See widespread flooding on pages 34 and 35.
4. Valley sides are often used for pasture. They were once forested. Taking away forests makes flooding more likely. The way this happens is shown on page 36.
5. **DAMS**, **RESERVOIRS** and **LEVEES** can be used to keep floods from farmland and cities. Why they are used is described on page 38.
6. Bridges are used to cross rivers, but they can partly block the flow of water and help to cause floods.
7. Water is often diverted from rivers to **IRRIGATE** fields and as drinking water for cities.
8. **WATER PURIFICATION** is necessary before river water can be drunk. Waste water (sewage) must be cleaned before it is returned to the river.
9. Lakes and reservoirs are used for recreation, but their main use is to store water, to prevent floods and to generate electricity.
10. Many cities were built near to the coast to make use of a sheltered harbour in the river mouth. To do this they have often had to **RECLAIM LAND** from a delta or estuary.
11. Gravel is often extracted from the floodplain and used as a building material.
12. Rivers are very important to us. You can read about the Amazon, Mississippi, Nile, Rhine and Yangtze on pages 40–46.

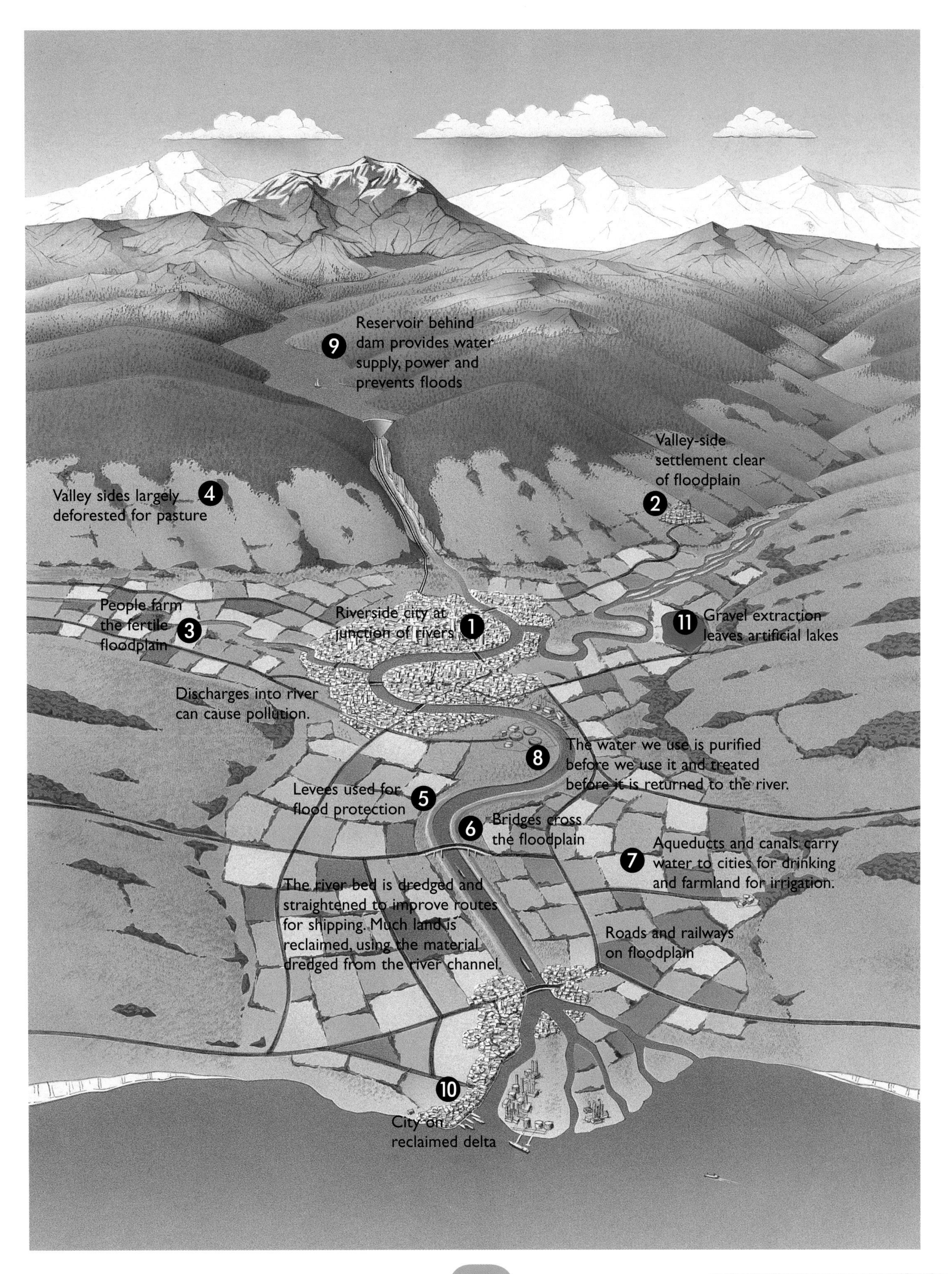
Reservoir behind dam provides water supply, power and prevents floods
9
Valley-side settlement clear of floodplain
2
Valley sides largely deforested for pasture
4
People farm the fertile floodplain
3
Riverside city at junction of rivers
1
Gravel extraction leaves artificial lakes
11
Discharges into river can cause pollution.
The water we use is purified before we use it and treated before it is returned to the river.
8
Levees used for flood protection
5
Bridges cross the floodplain
6
Aqueducts and canals carry water to cities for drinking and farmland for irrigation.
7
The river bed is dredged and straightened to improve routes for shipping. Much land is reclaimed, using the material dredged from the river channel.
Roads and railways on floodplain
10
City on reclaimed delta

Where rivers get their water

The water cycle provides rivers with water whether it rains or not.

Rivers flow even in times of **DROUGHT**. So where do rivers get their water?

The answer lies in the **WATER CYCLE**, the constant sharing of water among the land, the oceans and the air (picture ①).

Making clouds and rain

If you leave a saucer of water out on a window sill, the water will soon disappear. In just the same way, dry air soaks up water from the oceans as vapour. It is called **EVAPORATION**.

Vapour makes the air moist. Near the ground the air is relatively warm and can hold a lot of vapour. As the moist air rises, it reaches much colder regions high in the sky. These regions can hold much less moisture; so as the air rises, the vapour changes into droplets or even ice crystals. We see the droplets and crystals as clouds.

Inside clouds, droplets and ice crystals group together until they are heavy enough to fall to the ground. Then it rains or snows.

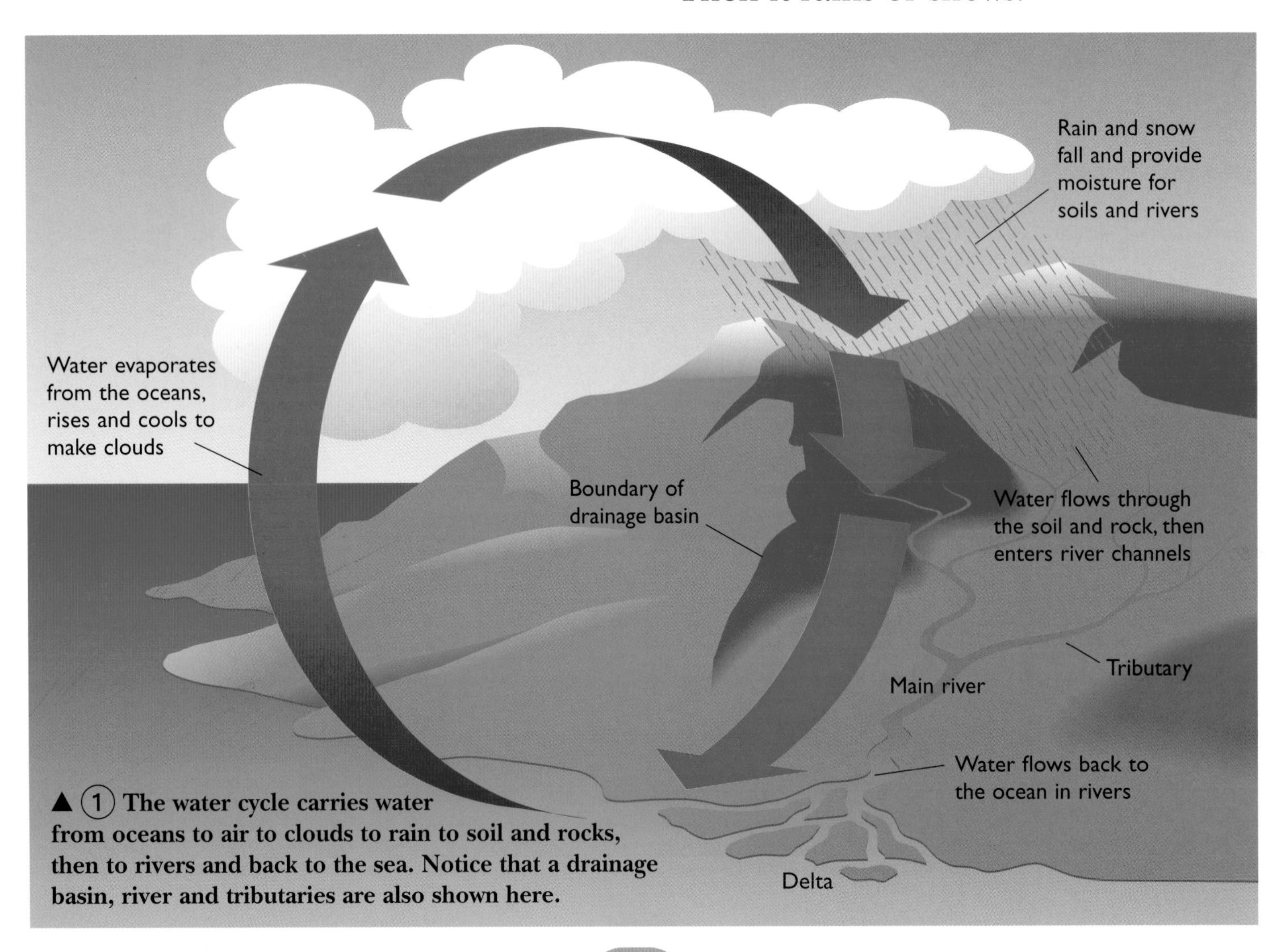

▲ ① The water cycle carries water from oceans to air to clouds to rain to soil and rocks, then to rivers and back to the sea. Notice that a drainage basin, river and tributaries are also shown here.

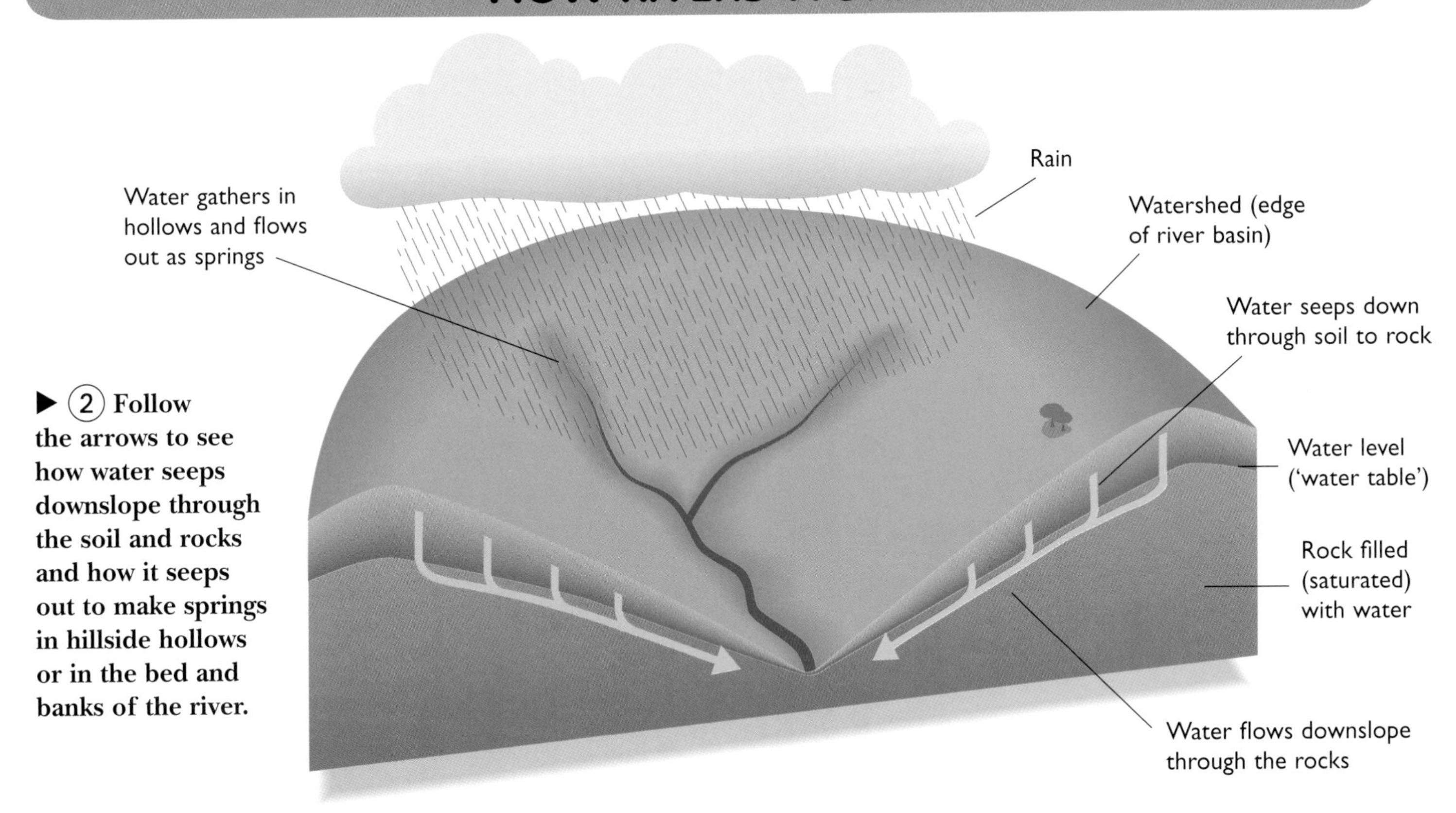

▶ ② Follow the arrows to see how water seeps downslope through the soil and rocks and how it seeps out to make springs in hillside hollows or in the bed and banks of the river.

From rain to river

Most rainfall seeps into the soil and moves underground – it very rarely runs across the soil surface. This is because soil and rock act as a giant sponge. Water seeps slowly down through this natural sponge, where much of it is stored (picture ②).

When many of the spaces (**PORES**) in the soils and rocks are filled with water, the water seeps out. Sometimes it forms a spring, but some water simply seeps out through the river bank or bed (picture ③). This water feeds the river between rainstorms. Water in the soil is also used by plants.

Finally, river water flows back to the ocean to complete the water cycle.

Of course, if there are several months without rain, the plants use up the water from the soil, and all the surplus water drains out of the rocks, so rivers will eventually dry up.

▶ ③ A flat sponge can be used to show how water moves through the soil and helps feed a river. Put the sponge on a sheet of plastic (such as a plastic bag), and bend the sponge and plastic to form a 'valley'. Add water slowly to the top of one valley side. At first the water soaks in, and nothing flows out of the bottom. But after a while a 'river' forms in the bottom of the valley and continues flowing long after water has stopped being added to the valley side.

How rivers wear away rocky beds

Two stages are needed to wear away a rocky bed: the solid rock must first be worn down into smaller pieces, then it must be carried away.

Water cannot wear away, or **ERODE**, the land quickly on its own. It needs some form of scraping tool to work with. That is why **PEBBLES** and gravel are important. But they are so heavy, they can only be carried by the fastest of streams and rivers, like those shown in picture (1).

▲ (1) When the river level is low, such as in summer, the rocky bed shows clearly. The air bubbles trapped in the swirling and tumbling water make it look white, and so it is described as 'white water'.

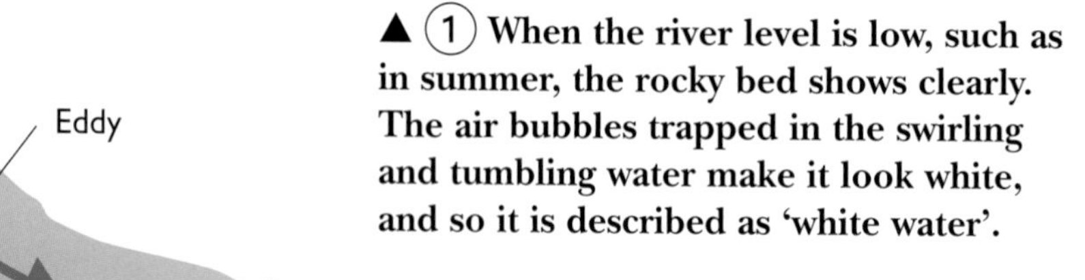

▶ (2) This diagram shows a side view of a fast-flowing river. The plunging and swirling water lifts the pebbles and gravel, then lets them fall back to the bed. Sometimes pebbles are swirled round and round and then they drill holes, called POTHOLES, in the bed. All of these actions wear away both the river bed and the pebbles.

Fast-flowing water

You expect to see fast-flowing water in mountains and other places where the river rushes through a steep valley. Picture ② shows what happens.

You can imagine the water as a kind of liquid sandpaper. The fast-flowing water provides the energy, and the pebbles and gravel (picture ③) are the material used by the water to scrape at the bed (picture ④).

▼ ③ These are the materials you might find on the bed of a white water river. The pebbles are rounded from scraping across the bed. The technical word for scraping is ABRASION.

As the pebbles and river bed wear each other away, small pieces of rock break free. That produces the sand you can see in the picture.

All these pebbles will, in time, become tiny pieces of SAND, SILT or MUD.

▶ ④ Find out how stones wear one another away by knocking a hard and a soft piece of rock together over a sheet of paper.

How rivers carry away material

Rivers drag, bounce, suspend and dissolve the materials they move.

Rivers are constantly flowing, although they flow more quickly in some parts than in others (picture ①).

But there is a problem finding out how material is carried. It is only safe to find out about the flow between storms. But when you look into the bed of a river at these times, nothing seems to be moving at all. How, then, do the materials move?

The importance of storms

Rivers move most of their material when the water is flowing unusually quickly, for example, after a storm.

Swollen rivers can easily push pebbles along. They disturb the river bed, allowing the water to sweep up **SAND** and **MUD** hidden below the pebbles and carry it away. As the river levels go down, the pebbles settle once more and again protect the sand and mud. That is why rivers suddenly get muddy after a storm, and why the water quickly becomes clear afterwards.

The river's load

A river can carry many sorts of material. They are called the river's load (picture ②). During a flood the load contains pebbles that are being rolled along, sand that is hopping along near the bed, and **SILT** and mud that is so fine it stays hanging in the water, giving it a muddy-brown colour (pictures ③ and ④). Some **DISSOLVED MATERIAL** may also be in the water, but normally it is invisible.

Water in a stream moves in mysterious ways. To find how it moves, tie different coloured ribbons to a cane, and then stand the cane upright in the water and let the ribbons trail out with the **CURRENT**.

You can easily see how surface water moves by using some simple floating objects such as hard dog biscuits, each a different colour. Dog biscuits dissolve and make fish food, so they are environmentally friendly, too.

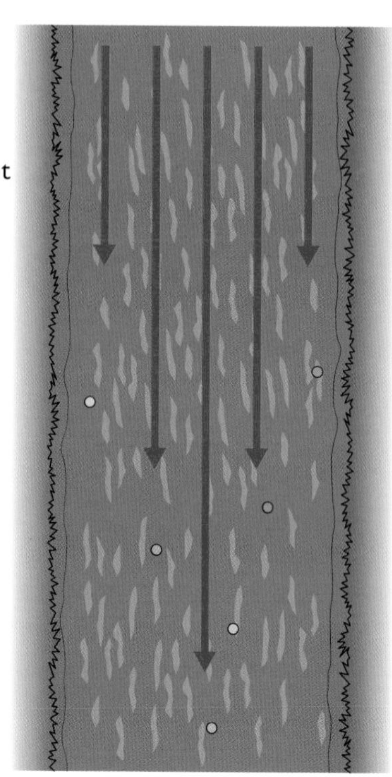

◀▶ ① **Here are two ways you can use to find out where the river is flowing most strongly, and therefore where the largest sizes of material are being carried.**

Never do this yourself. Always ask an adult to show you how this is done.

To understand how a pebble can become dissolved, try putting an antacid tablet in a glass of water, and then add a few drops of vinegar. The tablet will begin to dissolve, and soon all that is left of what was once a solid tablet is a cloud of fine particles. The rest has dissolved and is invisible.

Pebbles take millions of times longer to dissolve than an antacid tablet, but over time almost everything can be dissolved by the natural acids in water. Mud is produced by the chemical dissolving action of water on rock.

▼ (2) These diagrams show that many kinds of material move in a river, often at the same time. Together, all the types of material are known as sediment.

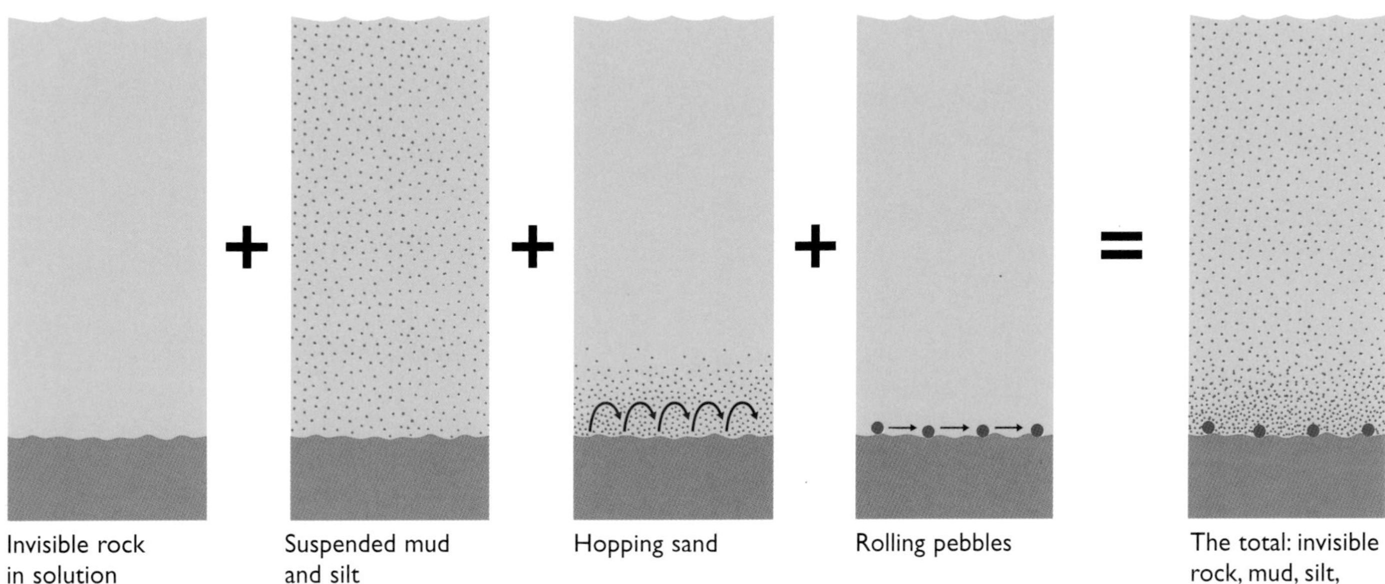

▼ (3) When rivers flow fast, the bed forms ridges, called ripples, just like the ones you find on a beach. Sand hops along near the bottom of the bed from ripple to ripple. Mud and silt can be swept along more easily than sand because it is held up – suspended – in the water.

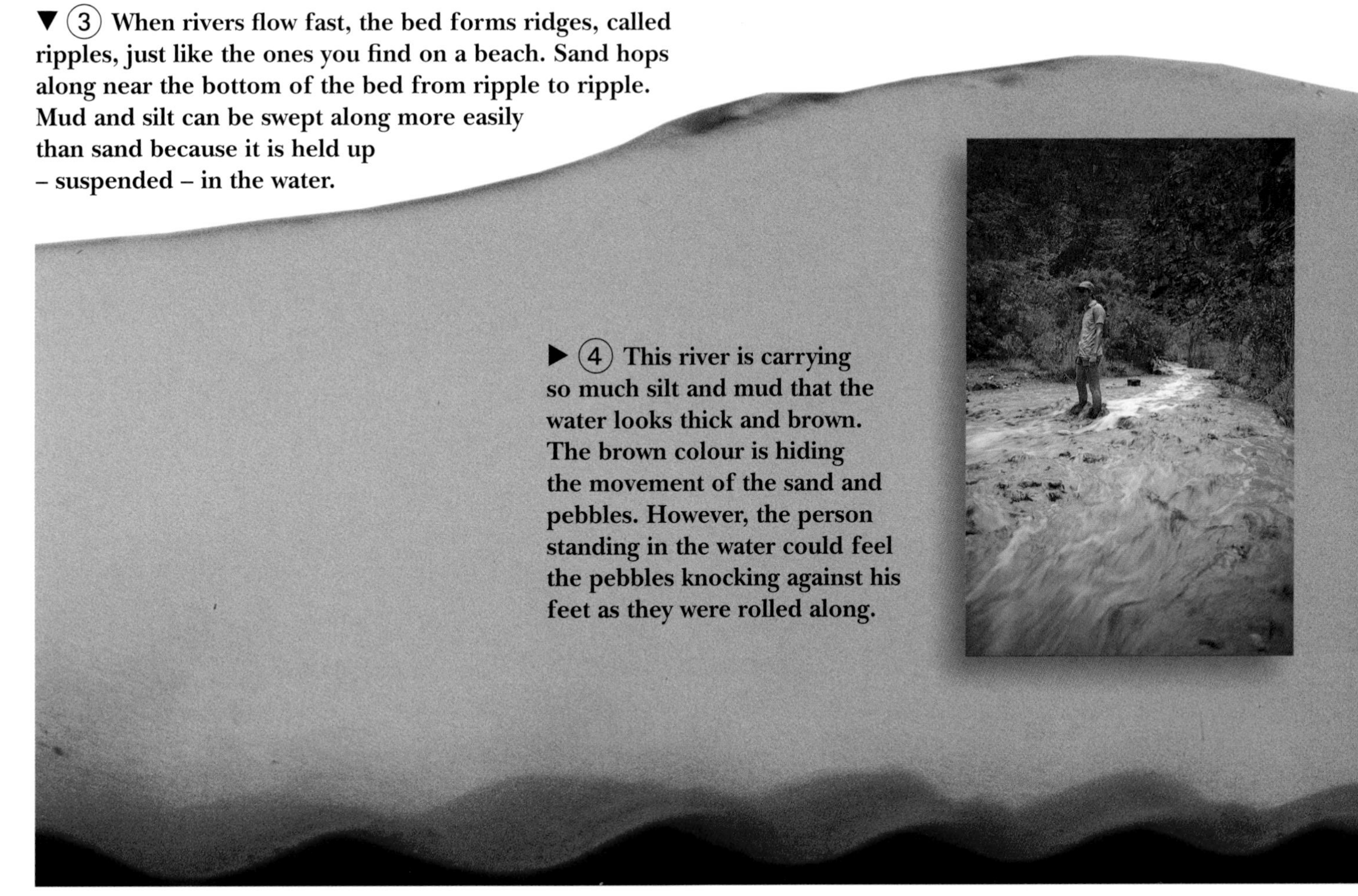

▶ (4) This river is carrying so much silt and mud that the water looks thick and brown. The brown colour is hiding the movement of the sand and pebbles. However, the person standing in the water could feel the pebbles knocking against his feet as they were rolled along.

Investigating rivers and streams

A river changes in many ways from source to mouth. Here are some of the differences and how to investigate them.

What happens to a river as it makes its way from its **SOURCE** to its mouth?

Picture (1) shows you what some of the changes might be.

Changes from source to mouth

Notice how the steepness of the river changes as it goes to the sea.

It is steepest near the source and more gentle near the sea.

If you were to pick up material from the bed of a river near its source you would find it is pebbly. If you picked it up half way to the mouth, you would find it was sandy, and if you picked up material near the mouth it would probably by muddy. So river materials get smaller in size towards the mouth.

There are other changes, too. Near its **HEADWATERS** the river is often straight as it tumbles down steep slopes. As the river gets to more gentle regions, it begins to wind, or **MEANDER** about, the meanders getting bigger towards the mouth.

Near the source, there is no flat land by the river, but towards the mouth of the river the amount of flat, floodable land – the **FLOODPLAIN** – gets bigger. This is matched by the valley sides getting gentler.

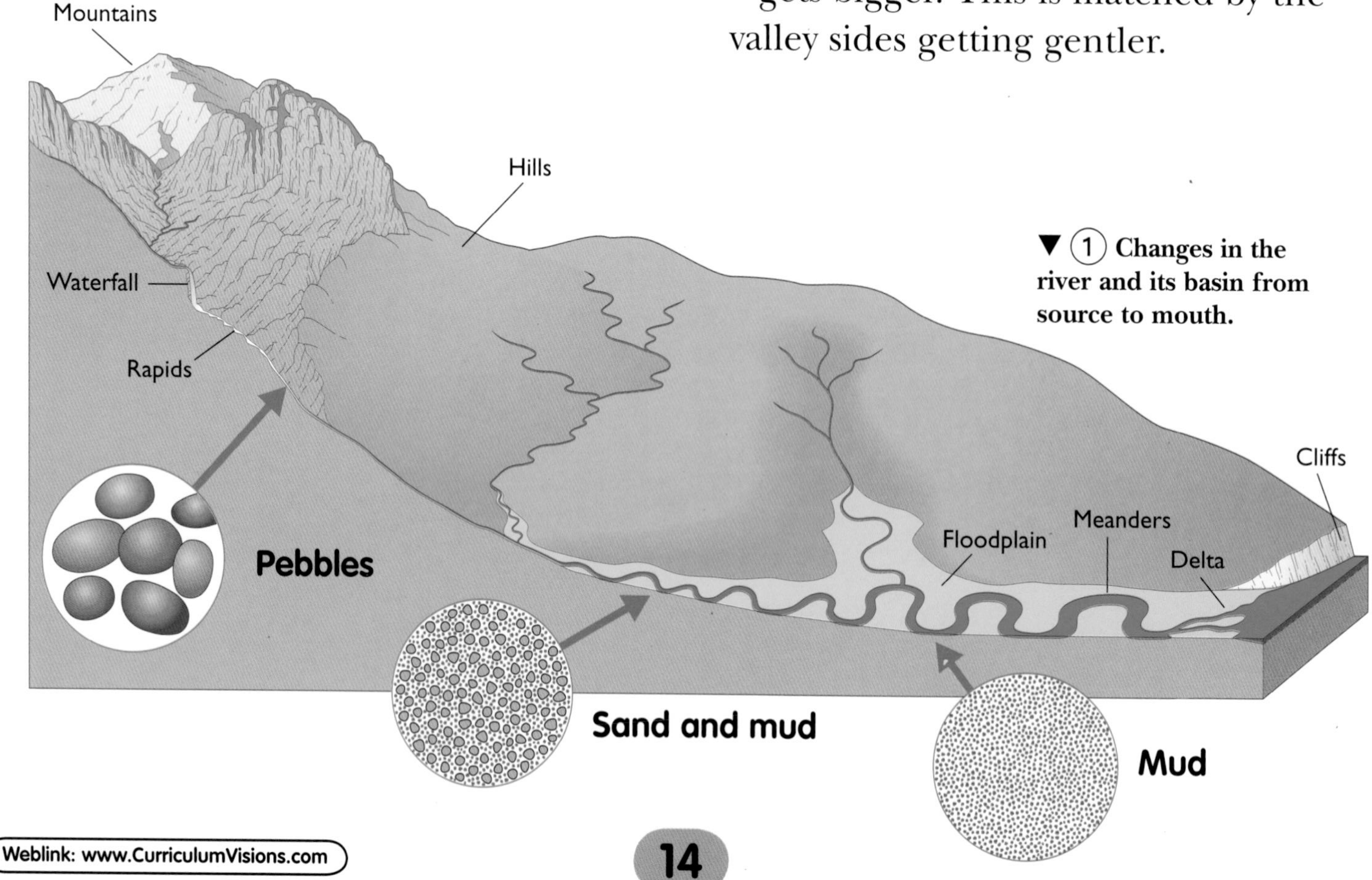

▼ (1) **Changes in the river and its basin from source to mouth.**

Find out what a river basin is like

You can investigate any river using a map. If you place a piece of tracing paper over a map and trace the rivers, the pattern you might see would be like picture ②. Here we have traced all the rivers of a basin and put a line around them to mark the **WATERSHED**.

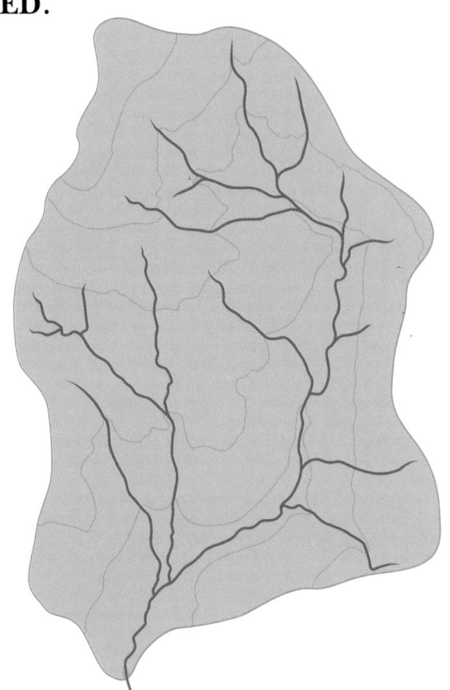

▶ ② Copying rivers from a map shows the route of the rivers. Drawing a line around them shows the river basin – the area from which the rivers get their water.

Measuring a stream

If you can visit a small stream, you can investigate changes on a local scale. For example, you can find out a stream's shape (picture ③). You can also dip an instrument called a flowmeter into the water to find out how fast it is flowing. Or you can use dog biscuits and a stop watch as shown on page 12.

Measure across the stream in several places to see if the shape changes. Then collect materials from the bed on the inside and the outside of a bend. Is your material sandy or muddy? Look at picture ① to see what this means.

▼ ③ You can measure the shape of a small, shallow stream using a tape measure, two stakes and a long, pole ruler like this. Write down the depth of water against the distance from the bank and then use the figures to draw up a side view. Do this on a bend. Then do it again on a straight section of channel between bends.

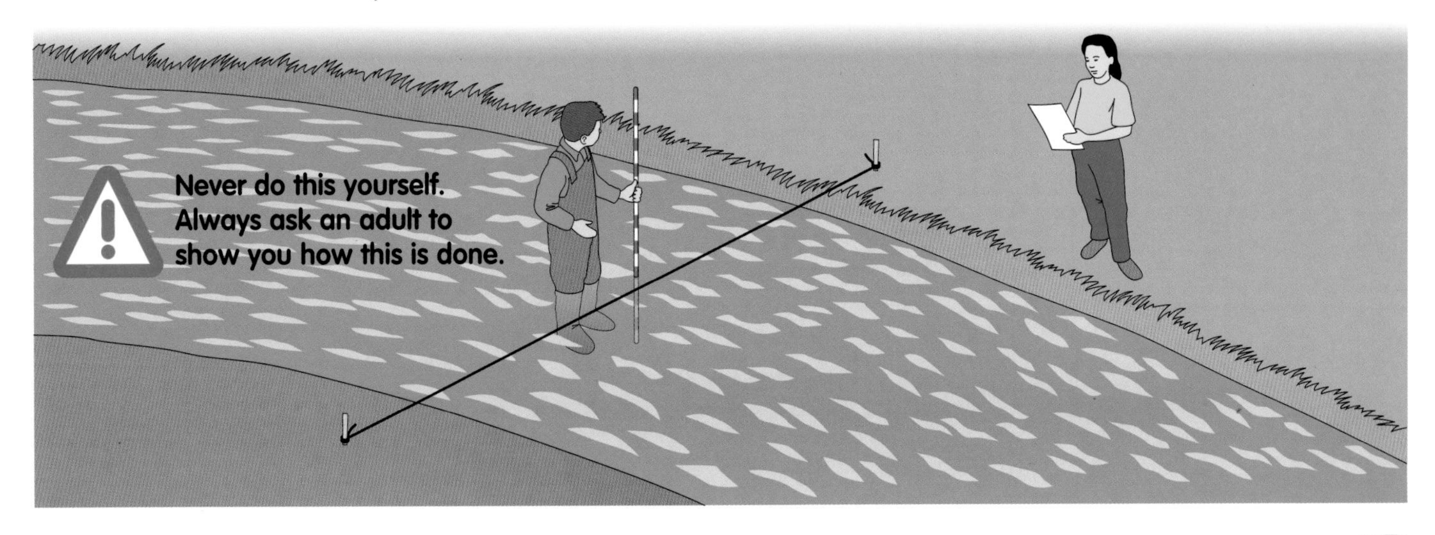

A side view of a bend drawn using measurements from the stream.

Waterfalls

A waterfall forms where a river plunges down a cliff.

A **WATERFALL** is the most dramatic feature in the course of a river. It is also unusual. Most rivers do not have waterfalls. That is because rivers only produce waterfalls where they flow over *flat* bands of hard and soft rock.

How a waterfall erodes

Rivers cannot easily cut through hard rock; but once they do, the softer rock below is rapidly removed.

You can see the way a waterfall works in picture ①. As the river water (and the pebbles it is carrying) falls down the face of a waterfall, it falls faster and faster. When it reaches the foot of the fall, it has great energy (picture ②).

The rock at the foot of the waterfall is worn away by pebbles in the falling and swirling water. This produces a deep pool called a **PLUNGE POOL** (pictures ① and ③).

As the plunge pool grows, it cuts back into the waterfall cliff (picture ③) and in time forms an overhanging ledge, or **WATERFALL LIP**. Eventually, the lip is left overhanging so much that it collapses under its own weight. The waterfall lip then moves slightly back, and the process is repeated.

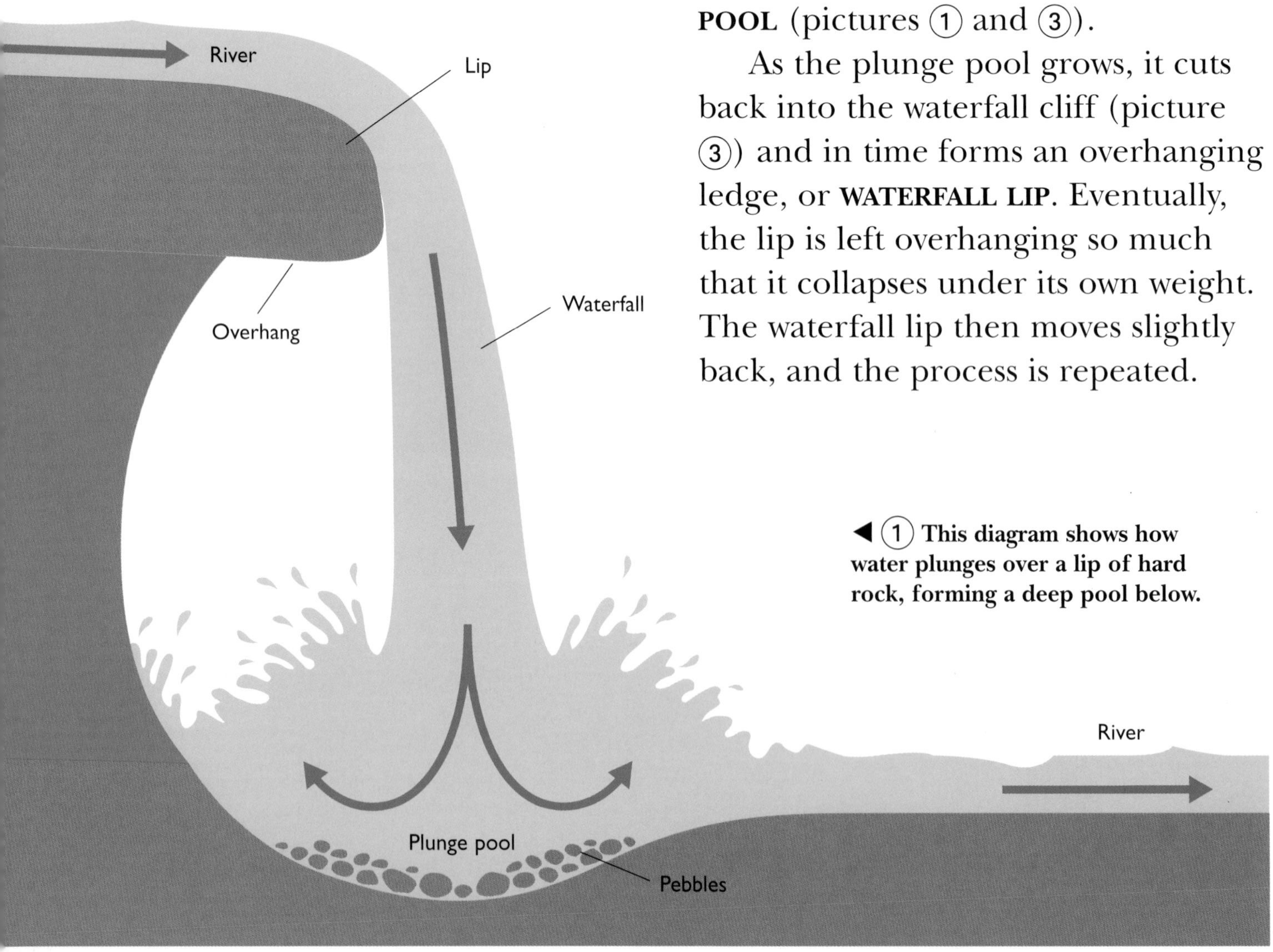

◄ ① This diagram shows how water plunges over a lip of hard rock, forming a deep pool below.

Often you can see a narrow **GORGE** downstream of a waterfall (picture ③). It marks the place where the waterfall used to be. In time, as the waterfall continues to erode the rock, it will form a longer and longer gorge.

Rapids

It is quite rare for rocks to lie in flat (horizontal) bands. More often the rocks lie at a shallow angle, and then **RAPIDS**, rather than waterfalls, are produced.

▲ ② **This is a view of the lip of a waterfall. You can see that the water is flowing quite gently above the lip. The water then falls to the gorge below. You can imagine that any pebbles falling with the water will crack against the rocky bed below and cause more erosion.**

▶ ③ **This picture lets you see what happens when the river's energy is concentrated at a waterfall. It erodes down and back, leaving a gorge downstream.**

Meanders

Most rivers make loops, or meanders, over much of their courses.

Rivers flow in **CHANNELS**. Most rivers cut a single deep channel in a muddy bed. This channel winds its way across the flat floor of a valley. A large curve in a river is called a **MEANDER** (picture ①).

How meanders change

As water flows around a curve, it gets thrown to the outside of the curve, rather like people on a spinning fairground ride feel themselves thrown outwards as the spin increases.

The river can scour its channel most quickly where it flows fastest, that is, near the outside of a bend. On the inside of the bend the water flows much more slowly.

▼ ① Investigate meandering by pouring coloured water down a gently sloping board. You will find meanders do not form just in soil, but occur when water flows down any slope.

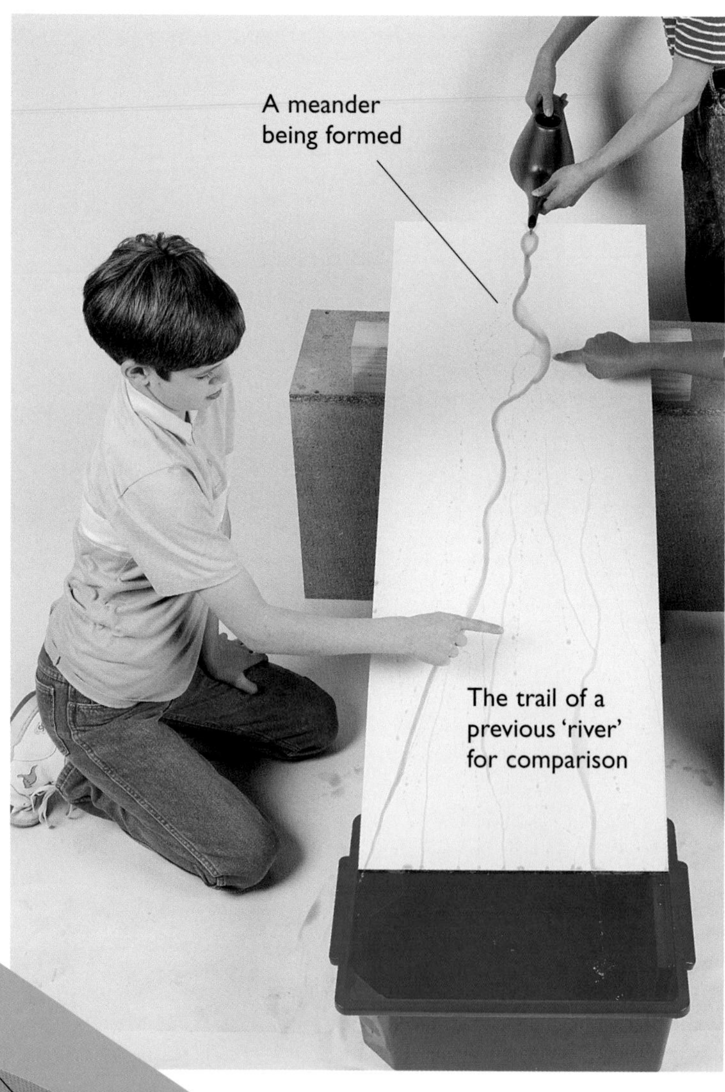

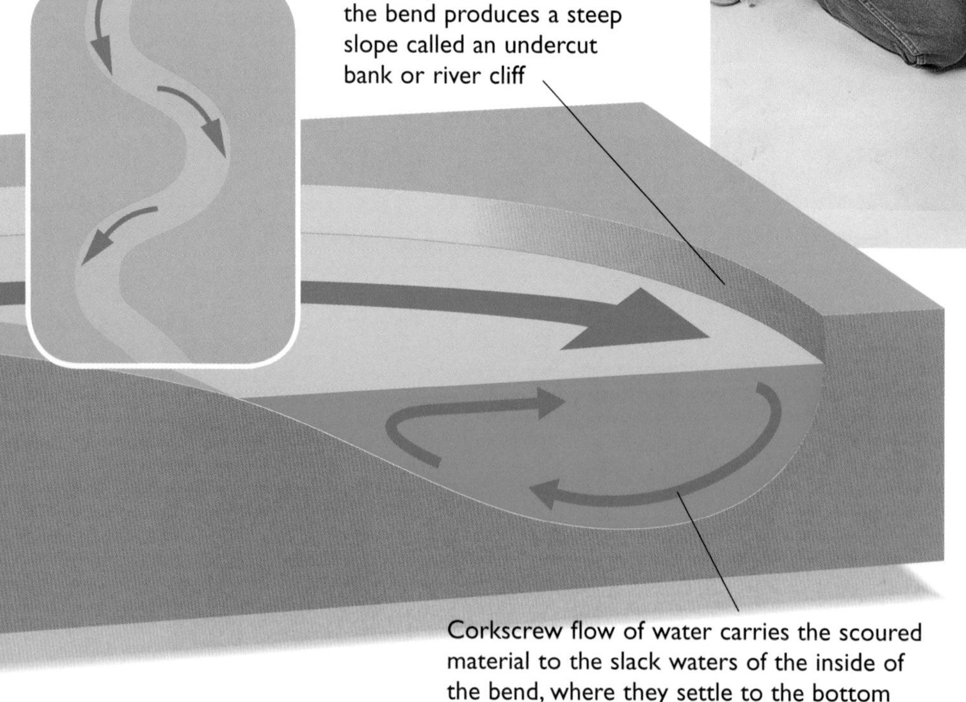

◀ ② This diagram shows the way that water in a meander flows around the outside of the bend. It erodes the bend and makes an undercut bank, or river cliff. The inside of the bend is not eroded and is shallow and gently sloping.

The difference shows clearly in the depth of the water. It is deep on the outside of a bend and shallow on the inside (picture ②).

As the river cuts into the outside of the bend, sand and mud settle out on the inside of the bend (picture ③). Thus a river changes its shape but keeps the same width (picture ④).

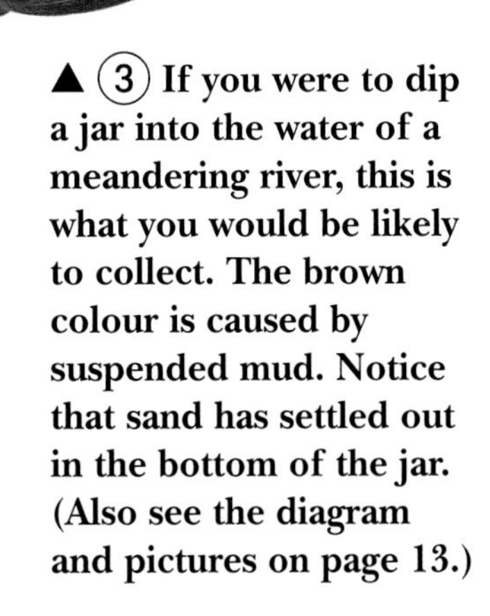

▲ ③ If you were to dip a jar into the water of a meandering river, this is what you would be likely to collect. The brown colour is caused by suspended mud. Notice that sand has settled out in the bottom of the jar. (Also see the diagram and pictures on page 13.)

◀ ④ This picture shows a meandering stretch of a river. The undercut banks are on the outside of each bend. Notice how the insides of the bends have plants growing on them. That is where sand and mud have recently been laid down.

Oxbows

Oxbows are narrow-necked loops of a river. Oxbow lakes are oxbows that have been abandoned by a river but still contain water.

A meander may grow into a very narrow-necked loop called an OXBOW. Oxbows usually do not survive long. This is why.

As a river goes around the tight bend of an oxbow, the oxbow acts as a natural brake on the water (picture ①). That makes little difference for normal flows; but after a storm, when the river is running high, the tightness of an oxbow bend tends to make the water pile up rather than flow freely.

At these times the river may spill over the neck (the narrowest part) of the oxbow and cut a new path, abandoning the oxbow completely.

An oxbow that has been abandoned is no longer scoured by the river. As a result, its ends quickly silt up and block off the oxbow loop from the river. However, because it is at the same level as the river, water still seeps into the abandoned oxbow, creating a small **OXBOW LAKE**.

▼ ① This diagram shows how a meander bend may become more and more pronounced until, during a flood, the oxbow is cut through and abandoned.

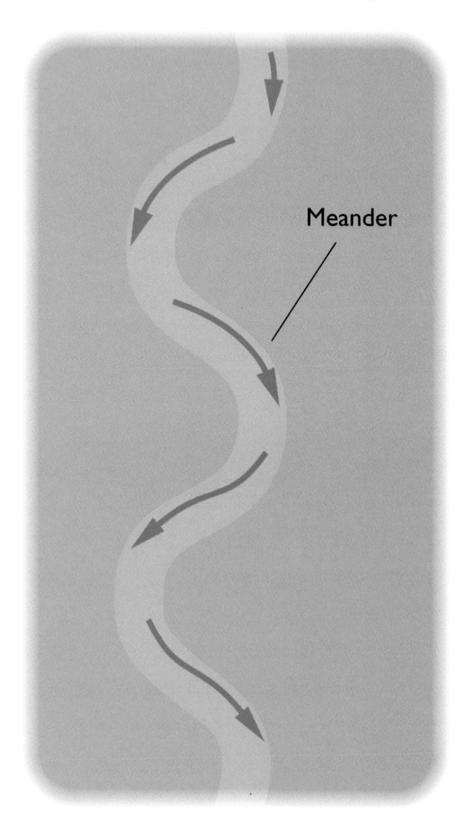

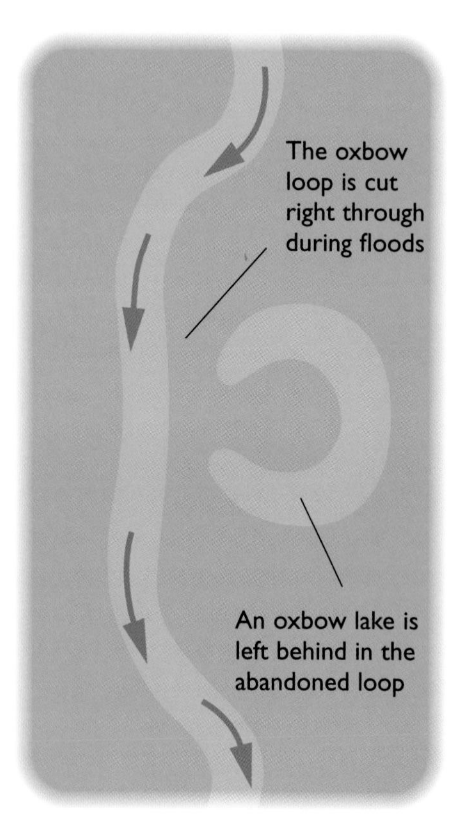

The best way of spotting oxbows and oxbow lakes is from a high viewpoint (pictures ②, ③, ④ and ⑤), but many also show up on maps.

▲ ③ An oxbow on the Forth River, Scotland.

▼ ② These oxbows and oxbow lakes have been highlighted to make them easier to see.

▼ ④ This picture shows an oxbow bend. Notice that it is an oxbow because the bend has a narrow neck.

▼ ⑤ A dramatic oxbow on the Green River, Utah, USA.

Lakes

Lakes are not formed by rivers, although they are commonly found in river valleys. Rivers are steadily filling lakes throughout the world.

A lake is a large amount of still water that fills a natural basin in the landscape. Lake basins are the only part of a river's course that were not formed by the river. Instead, they were created by some other natural process and have since been filled by river water to make a lake (picture ①).

Finger lakes

Most long, narrow lakes fill deep trenches in the landscape. These trenches were scoured out by ancient **GLACIERS**. Many of these lakes are in mountain valleys, where the glaciers used to be.

Because of their long, thin shape, valley lakes are commonly called **FINGER LAKES**. The Lake District, the Scottish Highlands and Snowdonia have many excellent examples.

Large lakes

Large, shallow lakes are usually formed behind natural earth dams. The Great Lakes (picture ③) were formed, in part, by a natural earth dam of debris left behind at the end of the last **ICE AGE**.

▼ ① This diagram shows the three important parts of a lake. The water enters, then slows down. The stillness of the lake then allows mud to settle and a DELTA forms. Finally, clear water flows out of the far end of the lake. Because lakes filter sand and mud in this way, they eventually fill up and disappear.

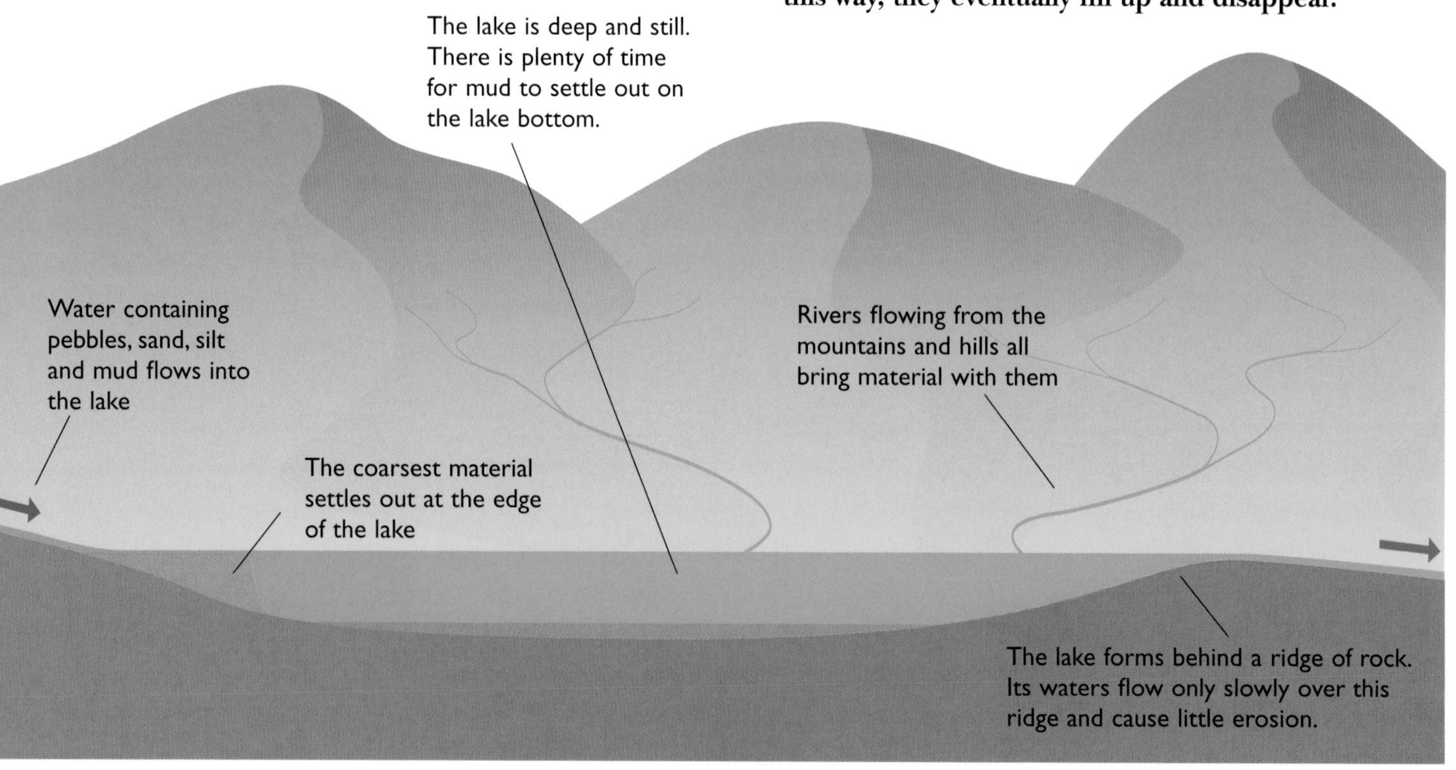

Large lakes are also sometimes produced when parts of the Earth's surface sinks. The lakes of East Africa fill parts of deep valleys called **RIFT VALLEYS**.

▼ (2) Here are two finger lakes in the Lake District. They were once a single lake, but a river on the right has carried silt into the lake, where it has settled out and formed a delta. The delta has grown right across the lake. In time, as more material settles out in the lakes, they will be completely filled in.

▼ (3) The Great Lakes on the United States/Canadian border are so large they can only be seen in their entirety from space. They were formed during the Ice Age. At that time the weight of ice pushed down the land beneath it making huge depressions. When the ice melted, the depressions filled with water. The five Great Lakes we see today are Lake Superior, Lake Michigan, Lake Huron, Lake Erie and Lake Ontario.

Deltas and estuaries

Deltas are areas of flat land that form at a river's mouth or in a lake. An estuary is a river mouth that does not contain a delta.

When rivers reach the still water of a sea or a lake, the river **CURRENT** slackens, and much of the material being carried settles out.

The heavier sand or gravel settles out first, and builds up until it reaches the surface. The new land it makes is called a **DELTA** (picture ①).

The river flows over this newly built land, so that sand and gravel are carried farther before settling out. By continually carrying material to the edge of its delta, the river gradually builds the delta out to sea or into a lake.

Shapes of deltas

The most common shape of delta looks like an opened fan (picture ②) and so is called a fan-shaped delta. It has a regular edge. This is the shape you see when a river divides into a number of more or less equal channels, called **DISTRIBUTARIES**. Each channel distributes a more or less equal amount of sand and gravel across the delta.

However, in some cases the main channel does not break up into distributaries. As a result, one part of the delta builds far faster than anywhere else. The shape of this type of delta is quite irregular (pictures ③ and ④). It is called a bird's-foot delta.

Estuaries

An **ESTUARY** is a river mouth that has been flooded by the sea. It is only a matter of time before enough sand and mud are brought to the estuary by the river to produce a delta.

▼ ① This side view of a delta shows its nearly flat top and straight, sloping front.

▶ (2) Fan-shaped delta. This kind of delta forms wherever channels spread out evenly across the delta. The example shown in the photograph is the Niger Delta, West Africa.

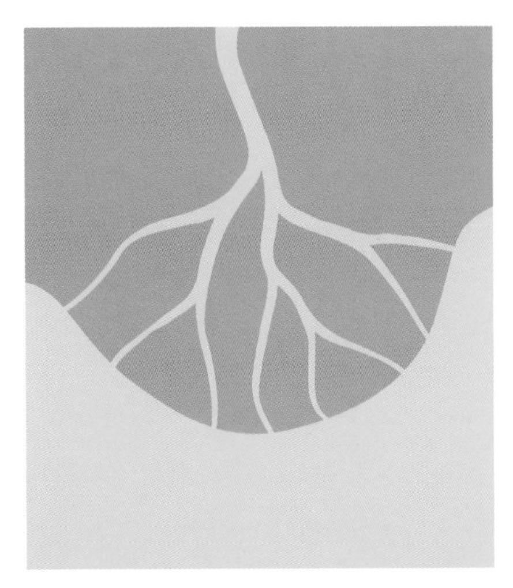

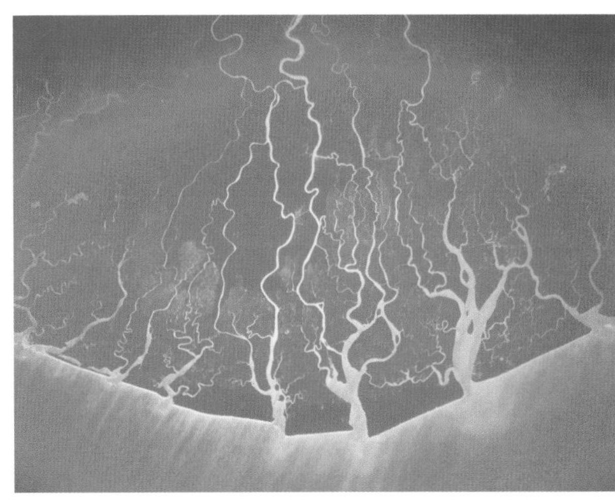

▶ (3) Bird's-foot delta. This kind of delta forms when a single main channel frequently changes direction. This example is the Mississippi Delta. The light–blue colour is actually sand and mud leaving the end of the delta and being washed around by ocean currents.

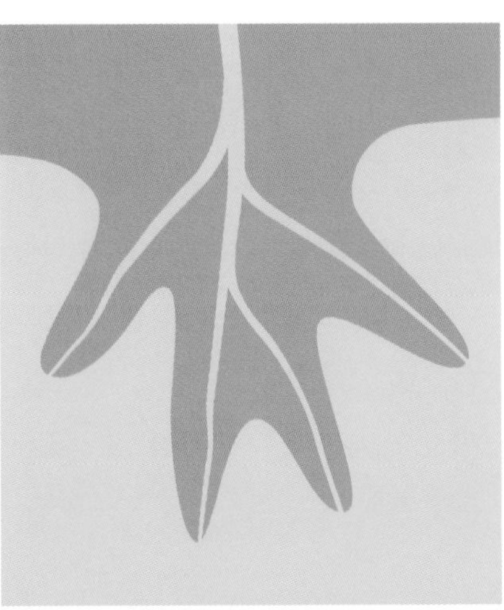

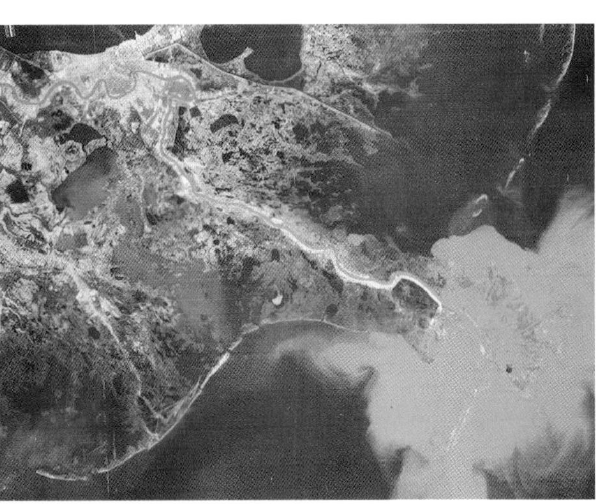

◀ (4) The bird's-foot delta of the Mississippi can be seen in this satellite view of the southern coast of the United States. Notice the great sandy plumes that stretch out into the Gulf of Mexico.

The delta of the Mobile River in Alabama is in the distance. Florida forms the horizon.

You can also follow the Mississippi inland and see its meandering course.

There is more about this river on pages 42 and 43.

Slopes on the move

Rivers are the 'conveyor belts' of a valley, carrying away rocks and soil brought down from the valley sides.

The river does *two* important things: It *cuts* down into its bed, and just as importantly, it *carries* away soil and rock that reach it from the valley sides. The kind of material the river receives depends on the steepness of the slopes (picture ①).

Steep slopes

Very steep slopes are bare of soil. You find them mainly in mountains and in deserts. During the cold of winter frost gets into cracks in the rock and shatters it into small pieces. These loose pieces fall away, rolling and bouncing towards the river. Occasionally large amounts of rock can also fall (picture ②).

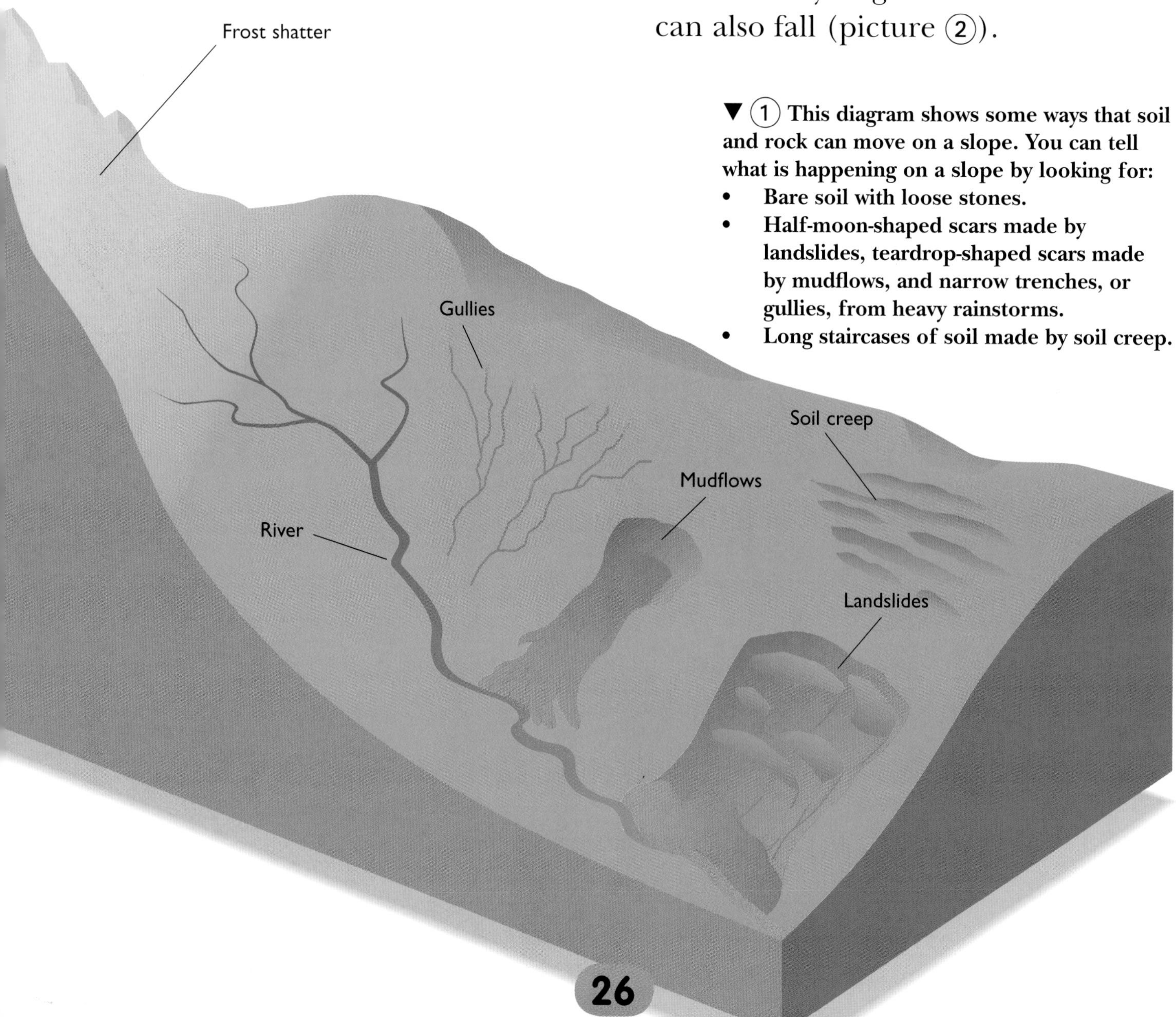

▼ ① This diagram shows some ways that soil and rock can move on a slope. You can tell what is happening on a slope by looking for:

- **Bare soil with loose stones.**
- **Half-moon-shaped scars made by landslides, teardrop-shaped scars made by mudflows, and narrow trenches, or gullies, from heavy rainstorms.**
- **Long staircases of soil made by soil creep.**

▼ ② This dramatic rockfall is in the Himalaya Mountains. A cloud of dust and rock marks the route of the rockfall. The leading edge is just hitting the river, causing a huge splash.

Moderate slopes

Soil forms on all but the steepest slopes. Soil is sticky and holds together well. Grass and tree roots also help hold soil in place.

However, when soil is full of water after a long period of rain, it can slip and slide suddenly and without warning. If a slab of soil slides, it is called a landslide (picture ③); but if it turns into mud and runs like syrup, it makes a mudflow.

These movements each leave telltale **SCARS** on hillsides (pictures ① and ③).

▼ ③ This river is cutting into the slope on the left (it is a river cliff on the outside bend of a meander), making it too steep for the soil to remain in place. As a result soil frequently slides down to the river.

If heavy rain washes over the slopes, then small rivers form on the surface. They can carry away the soil and form small trenches called **GULLIES** (picture ①).

On many slopes soil simply creeps very slowly down to the river edge under its own weight. You can spot where **SOIL CREEP** (picture ①) is at work because it produces long, narrow 'steps' on the hillside, making it look like a carpeted staircase. Creep also causes fence posts and trees to lean over.

Gentle slopes

Gentle slopes are not steep enough for mudflows or landslides to form. The soils are thick and hardly move. Nevertheless, rocks and soils are dissolved away, so that material is carried to rivers without us even noticing!

Gorges and canyons

Gorges and canyons are deep valleys made when rivers cut into the land very quickly.

Rivers flow in **VALLEYS**. A **GORGE** is a special kind of valley – with sheer sides (picture ①). It is formed almost entirely by a river cutting into its bed. A gorge only occurs where rocks are very hard and where the forces of the weather cannot break down rocks from the gorge sides. As a result, the valley doesn't get wider, just deeper (picture ②).

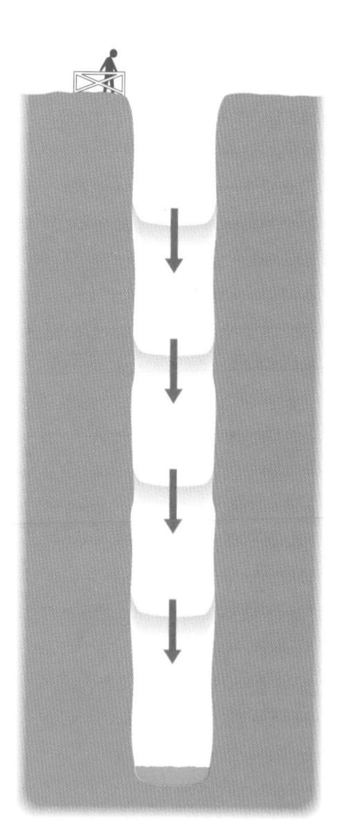

▶ ① This is the shape of a gorge. It is only being cut where the river flows.

Most valleys are not gorges – they do not have sheer sides. Even a **CANYON**, which is a valley with very steep sides, does not have sheer sides.

▼ ② This picture shows the main features of a gorge. Notice that the water flows across the entire width of the gorge floor, wearing it away evenly. The gorge also has sheer sides that have no plants growing on them.

How a canyon forms

Canyons are common where rain is scarce but falls in heavy downpours (picture ③).

The river still cuts down fast, keeping the sides so steep that soil cannot form and plants find it very difficult to grow, but the rainfall (and perhaps even the shattering action of winter frost) allows the sides to weather and shed material to the river.

The sides typically look like a natural staircase, with each band of hard rock standing out like the riser, and each band of soft rock making the treads. The world's biggest canyon is the Grand Canyon, Arizona, USA (picture ④).

◀ ③ The Green River canyons, Utah, USA.

▼ ④ The Grand Canyon was formed by the Colorado River cutting a trench into the Colorado Plateau. The land is made of many layers of rock, some hard, some soft. This unusual pattern has produced a spectacular canyon over 1,700 m deep and 30 km wide at the rim.

Hard rock
Soft rock

A view across the Grand Canyon from the South Rim.

Valley stages

In the upper part of its course a river flows in a steep-sided, twisting valley. But as the river reaches the sea, the valley widens and becomes shallower.

If you were to make a journey from the source to the mouth of a river, you would find that the valley had different shapes near its source, in the middle of its course and near the sea. People often talk of these parts of a valley as upper valley, middle valley and lower valley.

Upper valley

In the upper part of its course (provided the land has not been changed by glaciers during the Ice Age), a river is usually flowing swiftly, following a steeply sloping path.

The sides of the valley are steep and straight, and landslides, mudflows, and even rockfalls are common.

Look up or down such a valley, and you can see that the shape is like a letter V; so these valleys are often called **V-SHAPED VALLEYS** (pictures ① and ②).

Middle stage

By the time the river reaches the middle of its course, it is flowing down a less steep path, and the river cuts sideways faster than downwards (picture ③).

The expression 'V-shaped valley' comes from looking side-on at a steep-sided valley, as you can see here

INTERLOCKING SPURS

The river flows in the bottom of the valley

There is no floodplain (compare to the diagram on page 31)

Landslides and mudflows occur on these steep slopes. This fast movement of material keeps the slopes steep and straight.

▲ ① The main features of the upper course of a valley are shown in this picture.

▲ ② This picture shows a typical V-shaped valley formed in the headwaters of a river.

To either side of the river is flat, low-lying land that is easily flooded. It is called a **FLOODPLAIN** (pictures ③ and ④). It contains mud, silt and sand brought down from the upper valley.

The floodplain is formed as the river meanders swing from side to side.

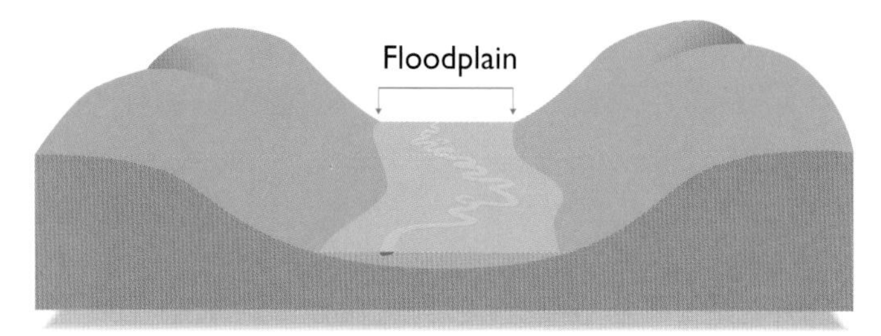

▲ ③ This diagram shows the middle course of a river. The landscape is called 'rolling'.

Lower valleys

The lower course of a river has a very wide floodplain and a valley with very gentle sides (picture ⑤).

During floods water spills out over the floodplain. Any sand and silt carried onto the floodplain will settle close to the river, building a wide, low natural earth bank or **LEVEE**. The lower Mississippi River has some of the world's biggest levees (picture ⑥).

▼ ④ This is a map that shows the landscape where the Missouri River meets the Mississippi River near St Louis, USA. The green colour shows how wide the floodplain is in this middle part of the river.

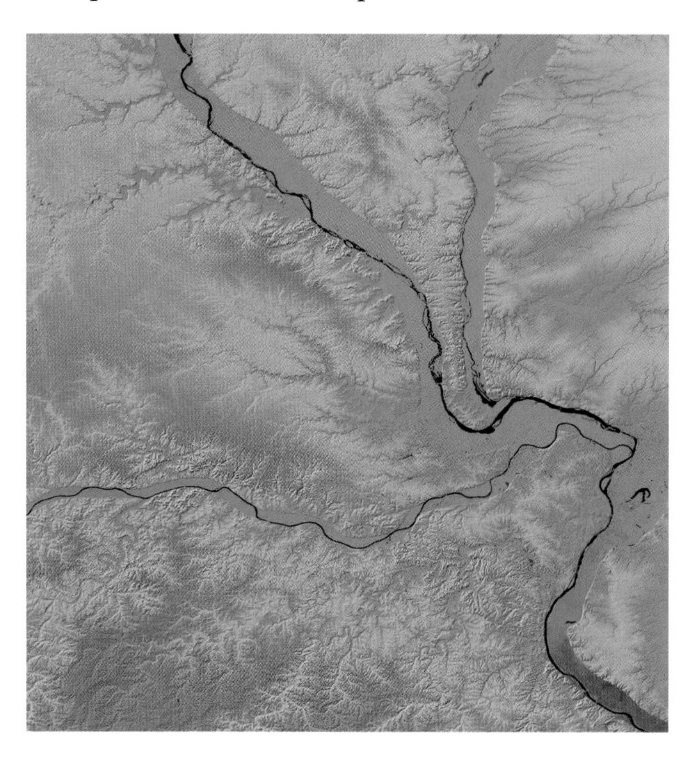

▲ ⑥ The Mississippi River near New Orleans, Louisiana, USA.

▼ ⑤ This diagram shows the lower course of a river. The landscape is almost flat.

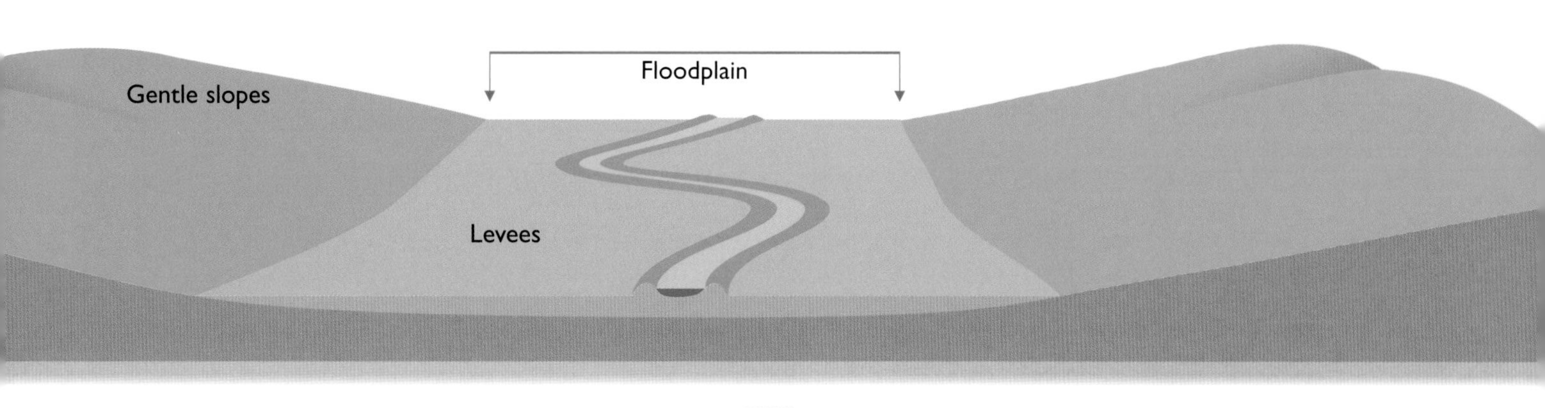

River and valley habitats

As rivers and valleys change from source to mouth, so does the wildlife that depends on them.

Rivers flow from high land, where they have stony beds, to lowlands, where their beds are made of mud and silt, to the sea, where rivers become tidal, and sandbanks and mudflats are common (picture ①). Quite different types of plants and animals are adapted to live on each part of the river's course.

▼ ① **The course of a river.**

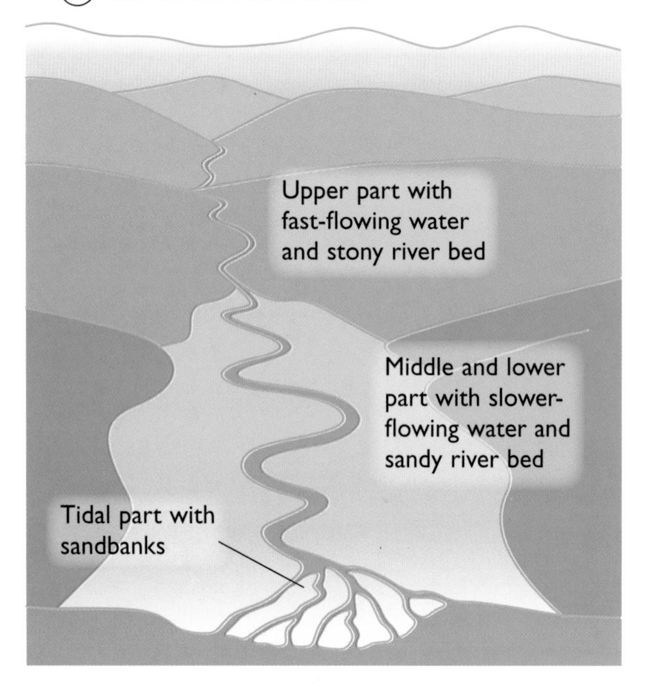

The upper part of a river

Rivers flowing quickly over stony beds would sweep many plants and animals away, so most river animals found here are strong swimmers or can shelter between the rocks (picture ②).

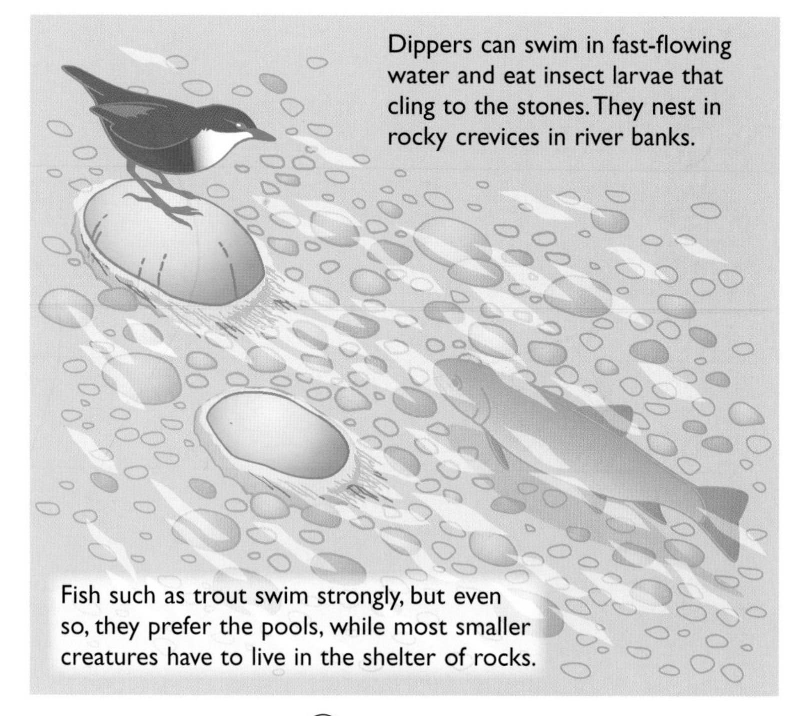

▲ ② **The upper reaches of a river, where the bed is stony.**

Here animals feed on leaves falling into the water or catch insects on or in the water.

The middle part of a river

Downstream the water flows slowly enough for sand, silt and mud to settle out (picture ③). Many animals have made use of this soft material to protect themselves. Animals such as mussels dig deep burrows. Rooted plants can also grow here.

Most small animals feed on dead leaves that sink to the river bottom. More varieties of fish are found here, including those that are less strong swimmers. River banks are soft and

▲ ③ **The middle reaches of a river, where meanders are cut in soft banks.**

▶ ④ **The tidal reaches of the river, where mudflats and sandbanks are common.**

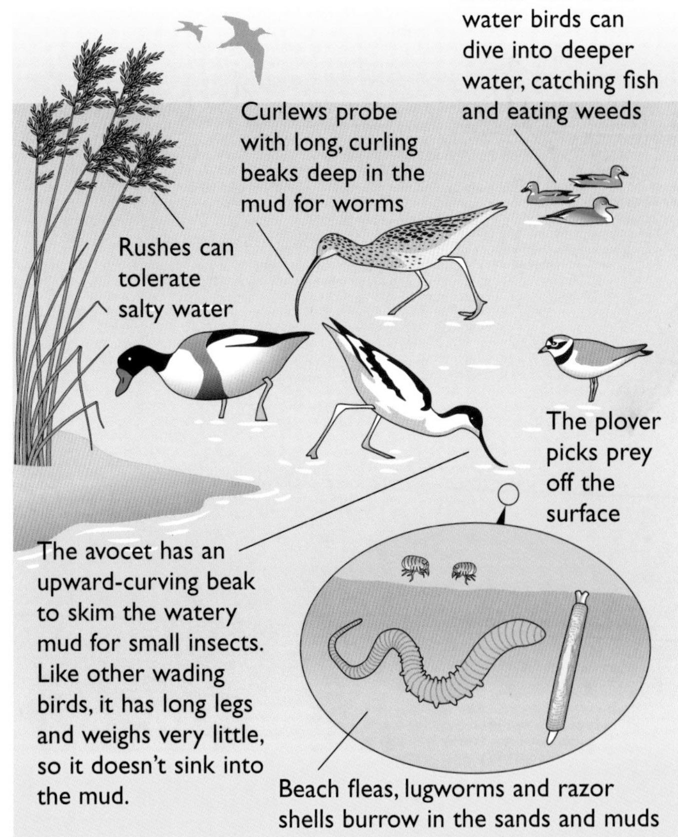

provide a home for burrowing birds like kingfishers, and mammals such as otters.

The tidal part of a river

At the mouth of the river the water is very sluggish and the bottom muds become thick. More plants can take root and huge numbers of burrowing animals, such as worms and snails, can thrive. Wading birds of all kinds are adapted to find the food buried in the sand and mud (picture ④).

Floods

Floods occur when rivers spill over their banks after prolonged or heavy rain. Often the whole floodplain turns into a shallow lake.

After a long period of rain, a heavy downpour, or when snow melts rapidly, the water reaching the river is so great that the channel fills up completely, and soon after the river bursts its banks. This is a **FLOOD**.

Different flood effects

Flooding has a different effect in each part of the valley. In the narrow upper course flooding can occur very suddenly because water is more likely to flow quickly off the steep slopes. There is little flat land by the river to store the floodwater, and as a result, the floodwater quickly moves down the valley. This sometimes happens so quickly it is called a **FLASH FLOOD**.

In the middle course the valley has a wide floodplain (picture ①). Water spreads over the floodplain, creating what is really a large, shallow, temporary lake.

The lake is slow to fill and slow to drain; as a result, floods may rise slowly, but they may last for many days.

In the lower course, where the floodplain is widest, floods take longest of all to creep up over the floodplain (pictures ② and ③). They are also the slowest to subside. It may take weeks for such floods to drain away.

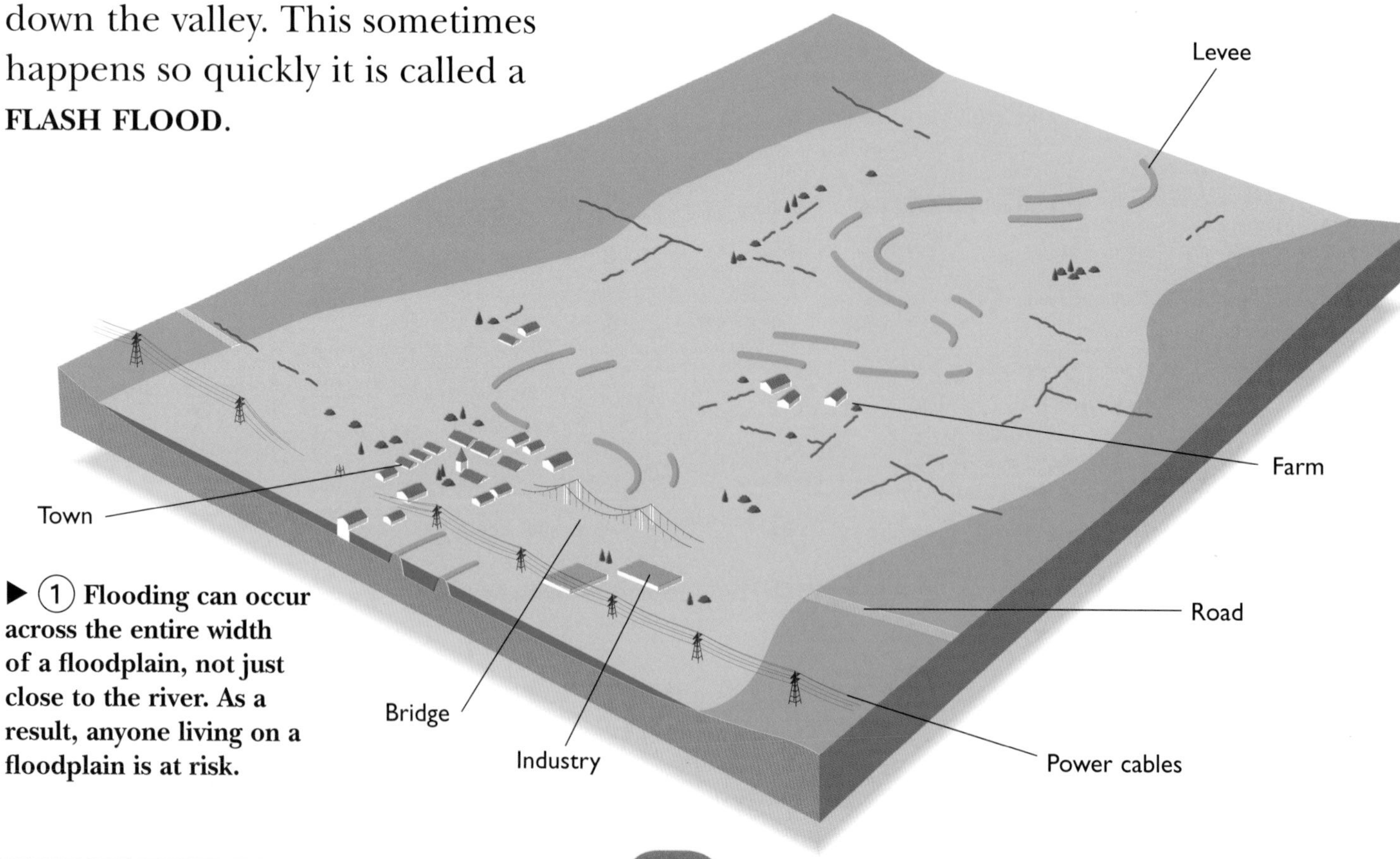

▶ ① **Flooding can occur across the entire width of a floodplain, not just close to the river. As a result, anyone living on a floodplain is at risk.**

◀ (2) You don't have to be within sight of a river to suffer a flood. It is quite common for floodwaters to rise 10 to 15 metres above normal during a flood, allowing floodwaters to reach very large areas. This picture shows a house half-submerged in a floodplain 'lake'.

▼ (3) This is a picture of the Mississippi River in flood in its middle course. The floodplain is very wide, and flooding spreads out over a very large area. Only the bridges mark where the river normally flows.

How people cause floods

People have made flooding far more likely because of the way they use the floodplain.

In some places people bring flooding on themselves. That is because they change the natural landscape to one with farms and cities, roads and bridges (picture ①).

Clearing forest for farms

Before forests were cleared, the soil was protected by the leaves of trees and anchored to the rock by their roots. But farmers often leave bare soil for parts of the year, and

▶ Farming landscape

▶ City landscape

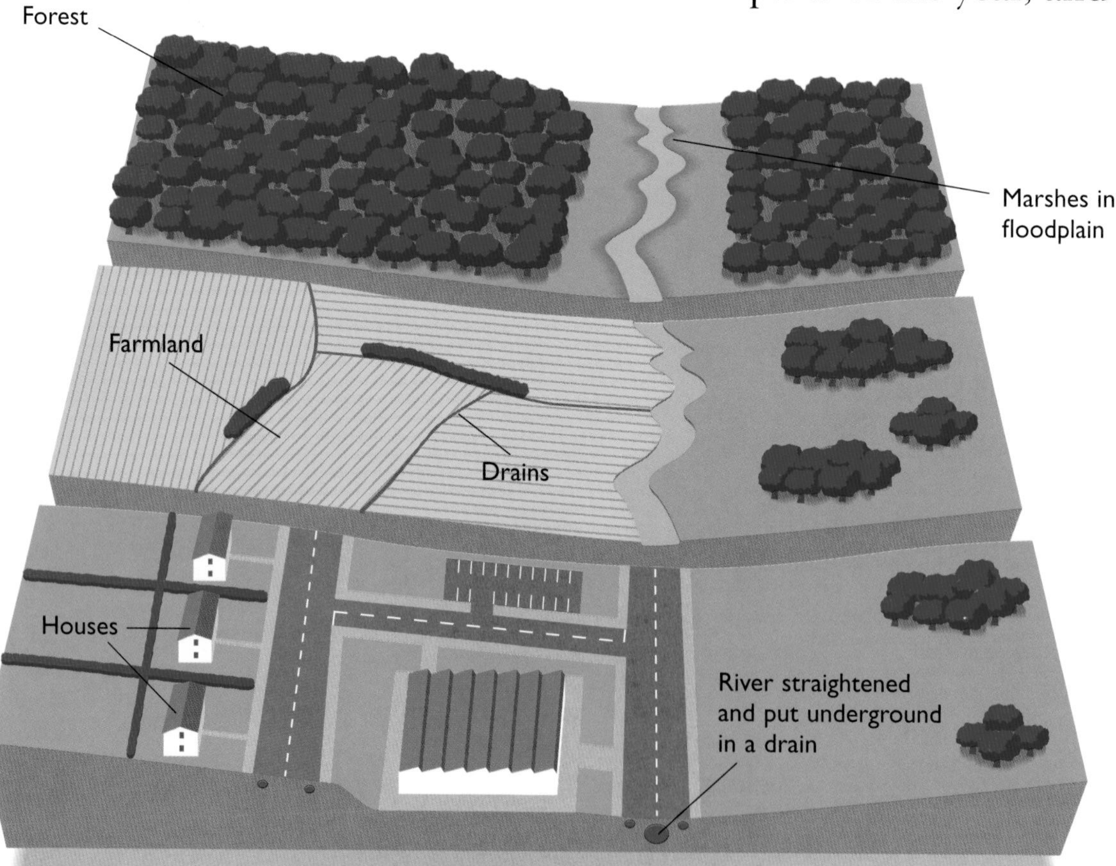

▲ ① This diagram shows how the risk of flooding can be made greater by changing the way we use the land.

◀ ② Flooding is often made worse when people take away trees and leave bare soil that can be beaten into a hard crust by heavy rain. Then the rain simply washes over the soil and straight to rivers. This picture is in Thailand, one of the countries most affected by loss of forests in recent years.

◀ ③ Los Angeles is a city that experiences short bursts of heavy rainfall. Buildings and roads have hemmed the rivers into straight-sided channels, while there is hardly any place for rain to soak into the soil. As a result, when it rains, flooding and severe EROSION are common.

then it is easily washed into rivers (picture ②). In this way, farming puts more soil into rivers, which settles out on the river bed, raising its height. That makes flooding more likely.

Building homes and factories

Towns, cities and roads have many waterproof surfaces. Rain cannot soak into the ground and instead it runs quickly to gutters. Drains carry rainwater quickly to rivers. All of these changes make flooding far more likely.

Changing river channels

Small rivers may be put into large drains while large meandering rivers are often straightened (picture ③). Both of these changes also make flooding more likely.

Building into the river

Many cities are built next to rivers. The river banks are reclaimed for buildings, making the river channel much narrower. Naturally, this too makes floods more likely (picture ④).

▼ ④ London's River Thames is only a third as wide as it would be naturally. Enormous amounts of river bank have been reclaimed. The narrowed river is much more likely to flood than in the past and walls have had to be built next to the river to stop the banks from overflowing.

Coping with floods

Floods cause great damage, and so much effort goes into flood protection.

If we live far from a river, we are unlikely to suffer from flooding. But many people do live on the flat land next to a river. As a result, they have to live with the risk of floods destroying their crops or their homes (picture ①).

Flood and mud

When many people think of floods, they think only of water. Anyone who has ever had to cope with a flood disaster knows differently (picture ②). A flood consists of *two* parts: *water* and *the material it is carrying*. Put simply: 'mud goes with a flood'. Mud sticks to everything inside a flooded house and makes cleaning up miserable.

How to protect homes

Many towns and cities and even farmland are protected by man-made banks, or levees (picture ③).

There are some other ways of stopping flooding. One way is to build a **DAM** and **RESERVOIR** along the courses of flood-prone rivers. Deep, narrow valleys are the easiest places to build dams. Extra river water can be stored in the reservoir until the threat of flooding is past. The water can then be slowly released from the reservoir.

Where dams cannot be built, the best solution is to make sure as much water seeps into soil and as little as possible goes into drains, for then there will be less water rushing quickly into the rivers.

◀ ① **Sandbags are used to try to keep out the worst of the flooding.**

▲ ② This picture shows the cleaning-up operation after a flood. The main battle is to remove the clinging mud.

▶ ③ These people are filling sandbags that will be carried to a nearby levee to help prevent it from collapsing. Look into the distance and see the thousands of people involved, and you begin to get a sense of the massive task in trying to prevent flooding.

Amazon

Location 5°S 60°W (South America); length: 6,400 km; drainage basin: 7 million sq km. The world's biggest river by volume.

Although it is not the longest river in the world (that title goes to the Nile), the Amazon has a far greater drainage basin than any other river. A fifth of all the flowing fresh water in the world flows along the Amazon system to the oceans, more water than the next six largest rivers combined. The average flow of the river is over 200 million litres a second.

▲ Sacred to the Incas, the Urubamba, some 3,500 m above sea level, receives water from the eastern slopes of the high Andes of Peru. Its waters drain into the Ucayali before eventually joining the Amazon over 3,500 km downstream.

The Amazon River system begins on the eastern flanks of the Andes. The rivers take a generally easterly course. By the time the Amazon reaches the sea, it has been joined by 1,100 tributaries. Some of these tributaries are large enough to be world-class rivers in their own right.

The largest tributaries are the Negro, Solimoes, Japurá, Putumayo, Napo, Ucayali, Juruá, Purus and Madeira.

▲ The Madre de Dios, one of the headwaters of the Amazon, is bigger than most other rivers in the world. With such high rainfall in this part of the Amazon Basin, river levels frequently rise and fall three or four metres in only one day, flooding the nearby rainforest and forming a raging muddy torrent in its main channel.

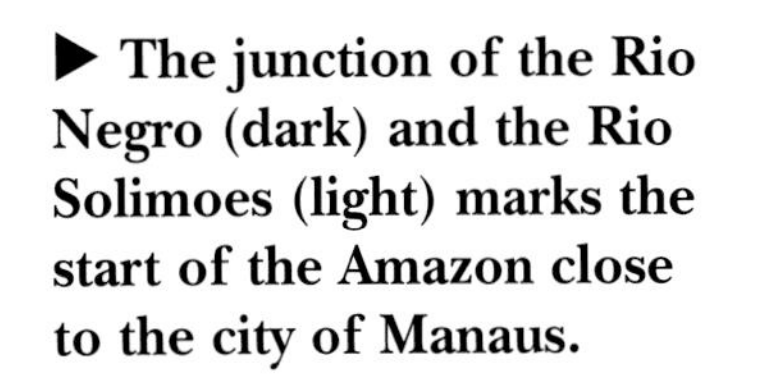

▶ The junction of the Rio Negro (dark) and the Rio Solimoes (light) marks the start of the Amazon close to the city of Manaus.

The main river channel is already 16 km wide 1,600 km before it reaches the sea. At its estuary the river is over 250 km wide, while the effects of the tides (a tidal bore) reach inland for 1,000 km – nearly as far as the city of Manaus. Manaus, which is accessible by ocean-going ships, is the only sizeable city in the Amazon Basin, although there are an increasing number of pioneer settlements.

Every year the Amazon floods, bursting its banks and covering 91,000 sq km in muddy water up to 10 m deep. The floods may last six months of each year.

▼ This is the mouth of the Amazon. The picture covers nearly 400 km in width.

The Amazon's headwaters are mountain rivers on the eastern flanks of the Andes. They drop spectacularly for the first 800 km and then reach the flat part of the basin. In its last section – about 3,500 km – the Amazon has a slope of less than 3 cm/km.

Mississippi

Location 40°N 90°W (US); length 3,800 km; drainage basin: 3.2 million sq km. Combined Mississippi River/ Missouri River system length 6,000 km. North America's largest river.

The Mississippi River, whose name in Algonquian means "father of waters", is the third largest river system in the world (even without the Missouri River) and covers about 40% of North America. Together with the Missouri River, it drains almost all the continental US between the Rockies and the Appalachians – about 60% of the whole United States.

▲ **The Lower Yellowstone Falls on the Yellowstone River.**

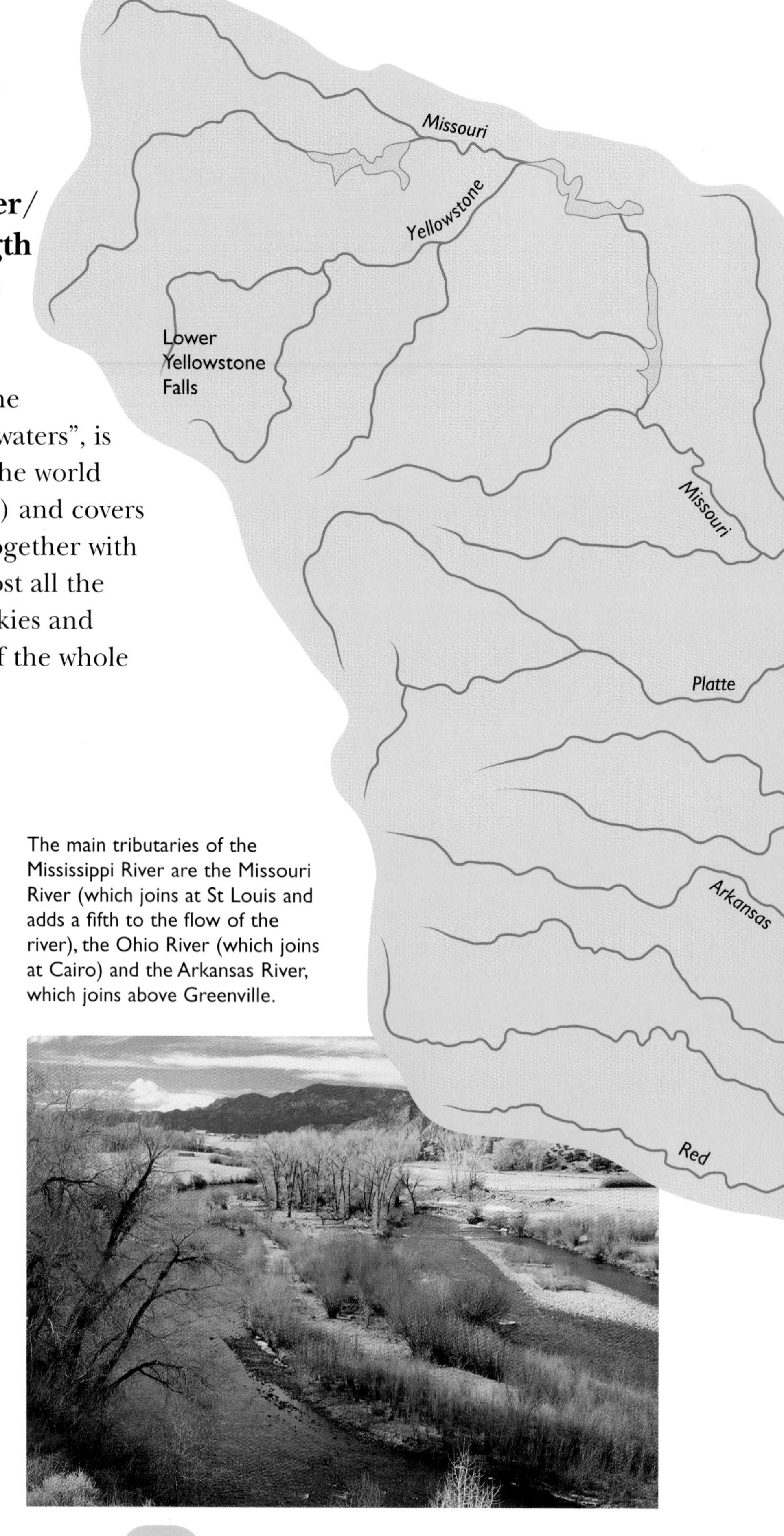

The main tributaries of the Mississippi River are the Missouri River (which joins at St Louis and adds a fifth to the flow of the river), the Ohio River (which joins at Cairo) and the Arkansas River, which joins above Greenville.

▶ **The Arkansas River as it flows through the Rocky Mountains.**

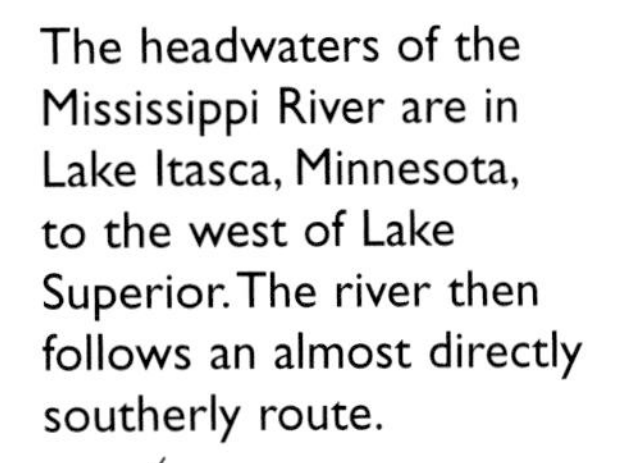

The headwaters of the Mississippi River are in Lake Itasca, Minnesota, to the west of Lake Superior. The river then follows an almost directly southerly route.

◀ (5) **St Louis, the gateway city to the West, showing a traditional paddle steamer in front of Gateway Arch, a memorial to the days of the pioneers who went west from here and prepared to follow the Oregon Trail.**

St Louis is just downstrean from where the Missouri River flows into the Mississippi River.

On its middle and lower reaches there are many natural levees along both banks. Here the river bed is often higher than the floodplain on either side, with the result that any breaks in the levees cause severe and widespread flooding.

▼ **Hannibal Dam on the Ohio River.**

▼ **New Orleans near the Mississippi Delta, protected by its high man-made levees.**

Mississippi
Missouri
St. Louis
Ohio
Tennessee
Mississippi
0 250 km
N
New Orleans

The Mississippi River makes a huge 'bird's-foot' delta that covers some 26,000 sq km. It deposits an average of 550 million tonnes of sediment into the Gulf of Mexico each year, so that the Mississippi delta grows outwards by up to 100 m a year.

Nile

Location: 10°N 33°E (northeast Africa); length 6,700 km; drainage basin: 3.3 million sq km. The world's longest river.

The Nile, famous since ancient times as the site of the ancient Egyptian civilization, is the world's longest river.

▶ ① **Cairo, the Nile's biggest city.**

The part of the Nile from Khartoum to Aswan in Egypt is in the form of a giant S bend, with the river's otherwise gentle flow broken by six rapids, or **CATARACTS**. Below Aswan the river flows in a gentle course to its delta in the Mediterranean Sea.

As the Nile reaches flatter land, it broadens out and is lost in a vast swamp region known as the Sudd. The Sudd acts as a natural sponge, absorbing water from storms and releasing it more evenly throughout the year. In this way the Sudd maintains water in the Nile throughout the year. The waters that emerge from the Sudd (now called the White Nile) make up just under a third of the entire water of the Nile.

The majority of the Nile's water, and the source of its annual flood, comes from the Blue Nile, which drains the Ethiopian Highlands. The rainy season in the Ethiopian Highlands lasts through April and May, and that is the time when the Nile flood is formed. However, because the river system is so long, the flood wave doesn't arrive in the Cairo region until October.

The source of the White Nile is in Burundi, beyond Lake Victoria. The source of the Blue Nile is in the Ethiopian Highlands.

◀ **Tisisat Falls just below Lake Tana in the highlands of Ethiopia. Lake Tana is the source of the Blue Nile.**

Mediterranean Sea
Cairo
Nile
Aswan
L. Nasser
Khartoum
Atbara
White Nile
Blue Nile
L. Tana
Tisisat Falls
Sudd
Bar el Jebel
L. Mobutu Sese Seko
L. Kyoga
L. Victoria

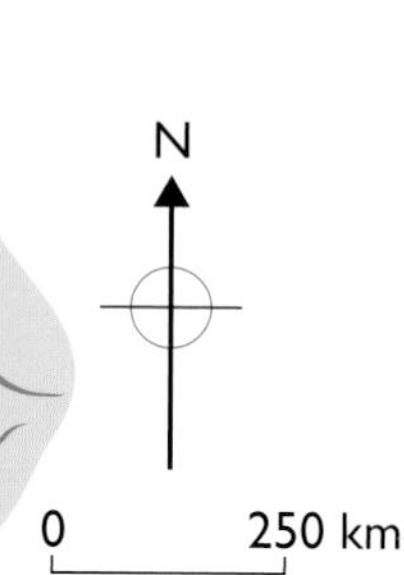

0 250 km

▼ **The green of irrigated fields shows the Nile floodplain and its delta in this satellite view of northern Egypt.**

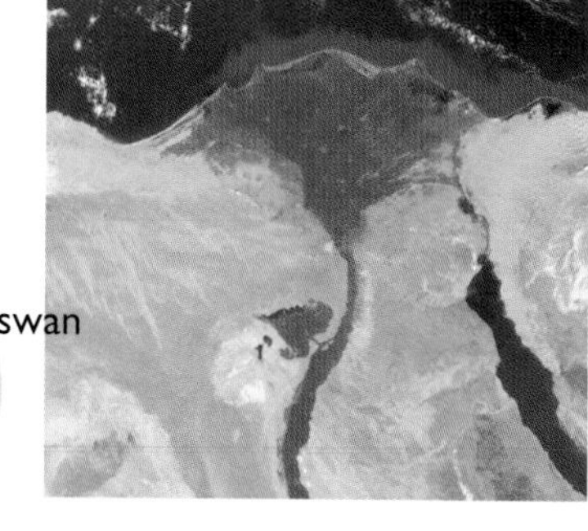

Lake Nasser is one of Africa's largest lakes. It is held behind the Aswan High Dam.

More than 3,200 km of the Nile are navigable.

Because the river flows for such a great part of its length through desert, it has few tributaries for much of its length.

Rhine

Location: 52N 6E (Europe); length: 1,300 km; drainage basin: 250,000 sq km. Europe's busiest river.

The Rhine is the longest river in Western Europe. It flows from a glacier in the mountains of Switzerland, through Germany, France and the Netherlands before reaching the North Sea.

More large cities line the banks of the Rhine than any other river in Europe.

Large barges can get all the way from the sea to the Swiss border. Sea-going ships can reach as far as Cologne in Germany. Many factories line the river to make use of the cheap transport that the boats provide.

The most famous part of the Rhine for tourists is the Rhine Gorge. People come to see the deep gorge cut through the mountains, the ancient castles that line the banks and the vineyards that are planted on its steep slopes.

Below Cologne the river flows over a flat plain and then right through the middle of the Netherlands where it makes a giant delta. This part of the river is easily flooded and huge earth levees have been built along the banks.

Rotterdam is the last city by the Rhine, and 50 km from the sea. It is the biggest port in Europe and one of the most important ports in the world. The Hook of Holland is a spit of land which marks the furthest point of the delta of the Rhine.

Because the Rhine has so many factories along its banks, it became heavily polluted and great efforts have been made to clean it up.

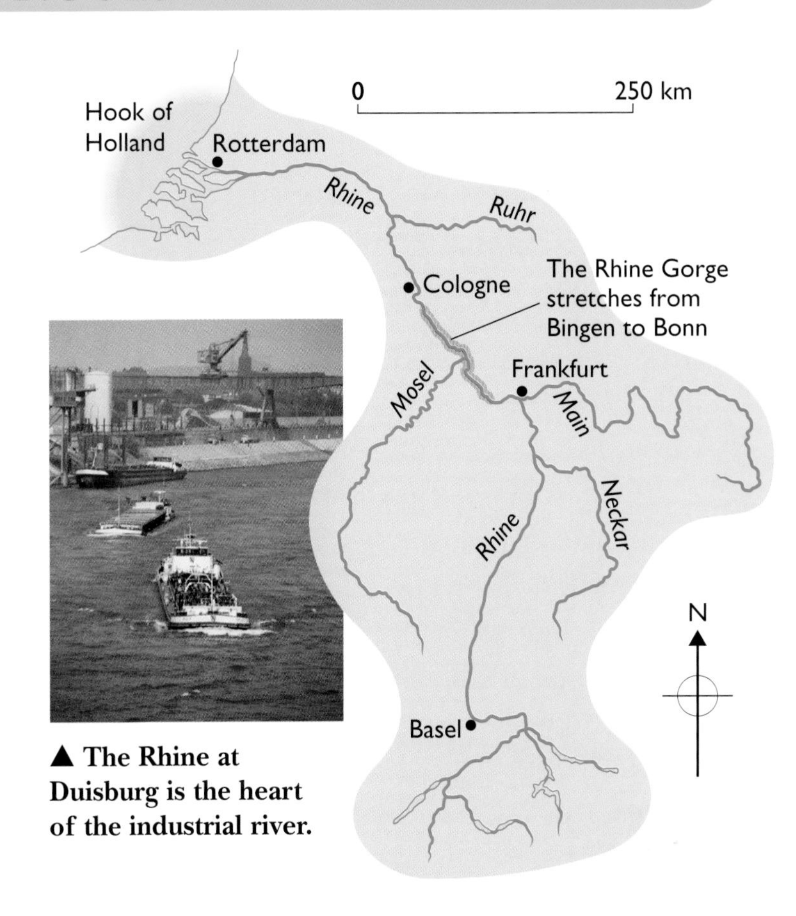

▲ The Rhine at Duisburg is the heart of the industrial river.

▼ Cologne, one of the biggest cities on the Rhine.

▼ The Rhine Gorge, showing the vines on the south-facing slopes and one of the ancient castles that used to guard the route. Barges still carry heavy cargoes along this important river.

Yangtze

Location: East Asia; length: 6,300 km; drainage basin: 1.8 million sq km. The world's deepest river.

The Yangtze (called the Chang in China) flows from the mountains of Tibet in central Asia to the East China Sea near Shanghai.

It is fed by melting snows in the spring and heavy monsoon rains in the summer. This is when floods occur.

The channel in the Three Gorges reaches nearly 200 m deep, making it the world's deepest river.

On its way from the mountains to the sea, the Yangtze flows through many different types of landscape. The most famous stretch of the river is at the Three Gorges. But the Yangtze also flows through large areas of very soft rock, and this is where it picks up such an enormous load of silt that the river is always a yellow or brown colour. When the river reaches the sea it drops the silt, building its delta outwards at 3 km a century.

The Yangtze has over 30,000 km of navigable waterway. Ocean-going vessels can reach 1,000 km from the coast. This contrasts with many of China's other rivers, and it makes the Yangtze more useful for water traffic than all the other rivers in China combined.

Many people have been attracted to settle by the river, and some of China's largest cities were founded at crossing points.

▲ A hydrofoil speeds upstream from Yichang on the silt-laden waters of the Yangtze. Behind it in the haze towers the enormous Three Gorges Dam. When finished, the dam will be over 180 m high and some 2 km wide, making it the biggest dam in the world.

The dam has been built just below the Three Gorges (below). The water will rise up the sides of the gorges making a reservoir that will spread 650 km upstream and changing the landscape forever.

The Yangtze has an enormous potential for generating electricity. Nearly half of all China's hydroelectric power is already produced from power stations on the river, but the potential is much greater. Now the Three Gorges Dam, one of the largest dam projects in the world, will provide even more power.

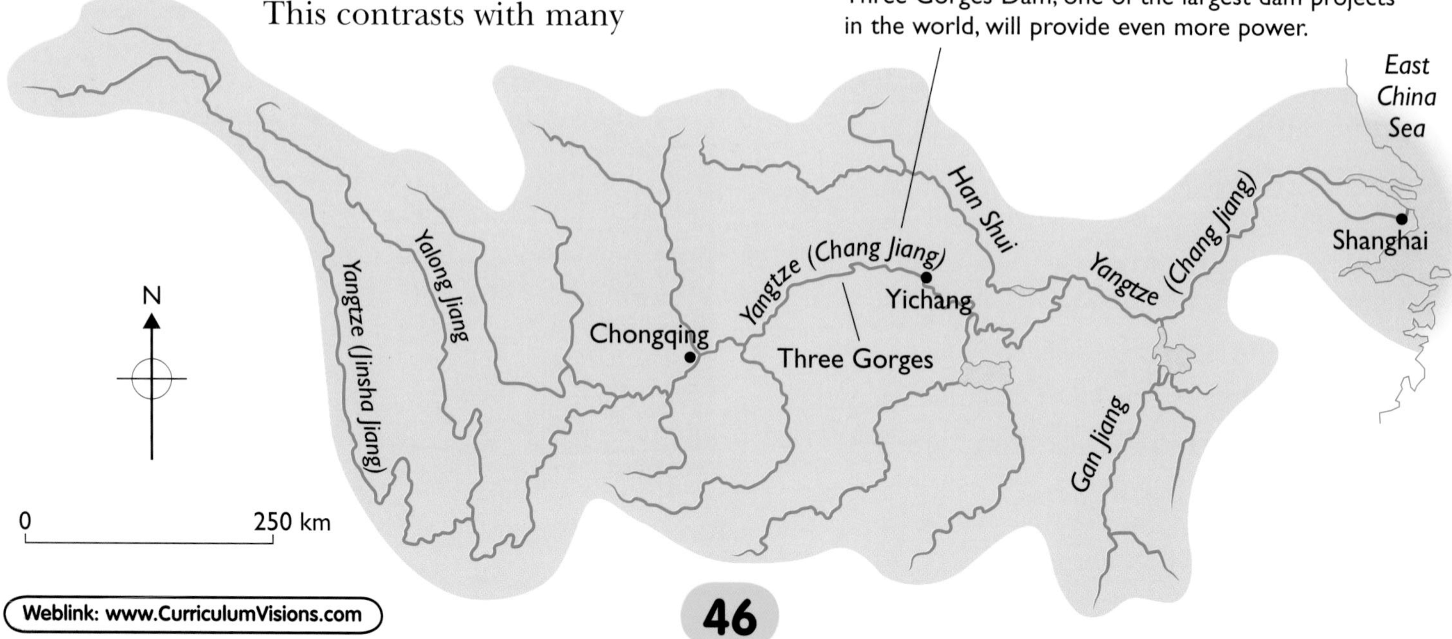

Glossary

ABRASION The wearing away of a river bed by the scouring action of pebbles.

CANYON A very steep-sided river valley, usually found in desert areas.

CATARACT A series of rapids or waterfalls on a large river.

CHANNEL The trench in which a river flows. If a channel's bed and banks are made of mud, it will be deep; if they are made of pebbles, the channel will be shallow and contain many islands.

CLIFF A vertical slope, usually with a rocky face.

CURRENT The swiftest part of a stream or river.

DAM A man-made barrier across a river designed to make an artificial lake.

DELTA The fan-shaped area of land that builds up where a river enters a sea or lake.

DEPOSIT To allow to settle out. Rivers deposit sand, silt, mud and pebbles on their beds. They deposit silt, sand and mud on their floodplains.

DISSOLVED MATERIAL Rock that has been dissolved and put into solution.

DISTRIBUTARIES Small channels that flow over a delta.

DROUGHT A long period without rain.

ERODE/EROSION The wearing away and removal of land.

ESTUARY The coastal part of a drowned river valley containing sea water.

EVAPORATION When liquid water turns into vapour.

FINGER LAKE A long, narrow lake in a mountain valley.

FLASH FLOOD A flood that happens within a few minutes after a heavy downpour of rain.

FLOOD When a river bursts its banks.

FLOODPLAIN The flat land to either side of a river that is made of materials deposited by the river during floods.

GLACIER A long finger of ice that partly fills a valley.

GORGE A narrow river valley with vertical sides.

GULLIES Small trenches in the soil formed by running water.

HEADWATERS The place where the river has its source.

ICE AGE A period of time, beginning about 2 million years ago, when it was common, from time to time, for glaciers to surge down from mountains and form ice sheets. At present, glaciers and ice sheets have shrunk back, but it is likely they will grow again.

INTERLOCKING SPURS Parts of the valley sides that jut out part way across the valley, alternately from the left- and right-hand sides.

IRRIGATION Watering farmland.

LAKE A natural hollow in which river water is stored.

LEVEE A natural or man-made earth bank near and parallel to the river channel.

MEANDER A big curve in a river's course that only forms on floodplains.

MUD Tiny minerals made by the chemical rotting of rock in water are called clay. The clay readily sticks together to form mud.

OXBOW A word used to describe a loop in a river which nearly doubles back on itself.

OXBOW LAKE An abandoned loop of river.

PEBBLE A smooth stone that has been worn by movement in a river.

PLUNGE POOL The hollow scoured out by pebbles at the bottom of a waterfall.

PORES Tiny gaps between particles of soil and rock that allow water to seep through soil and rock, and so find its way to the river.

POTHOLE A hole drilled in the bed of a river by swirling pebbles. (Do not confuse a river pothole with a caver's word for a hole where water sinks into the ground which is also called a pothole, or more correctly, a swallow hole).

RAPIDS A swift flow of water over bands of hard rock that jut up from the river bed.

RECLAIM LAND To turn land that was once river bed into land for living on.

RESERVOIR An artificial lake held behind a dam.

RIFT VALLEYS Valleys caused by a downwards movement of part of the Earth's surface.

RIVER BASIN The area drained by a river and its tributaries.

SAND Fragments of rock about the same size as sugar grains.

SCAR A bare patch of ground showing where soil used to be.

SILT Fragments of rock about the same size as dust.

SOIL CREEP The slow movement of soil down a steep slope.

SOURCE The place where the river starts, perhaps in a spring.

SPRING A place where water seeps out of soil or rock to make a stream.

TRIBUTARIES Small parts, or branches, of a stream or river that join others to make a larger river.

VALLEY A long trench in the landscape. In a river valley, sides slope down to the river channel.

V-SHAPED VALLEY A river valley with straight sides that look like a letter V.

WATER CYCLE The constant flow of water from rivers to the sea to the air and back to the land again.

WATER PURIFICATION Making river water fit to drink.

WATERFALL A fall of water over a ledge of hard rock.

WATERFALL LIP The ledge of hard rock at a waterfall.

WATERSHED The line that separates one river basin from another.

Index